# LET'S LEARN ABOUT...
# THE LAND

## Teacher's Guide

## CBeebies

## K2

**Pearson Education Limited**
KAO Two, KAO Park, Harlow, Essex, CM17 9NA, England
and Associated Companies around the world.

© Pearson Education Limited 2020

The right of Rhiannon S. Ball to be identified as author of this Work has been asserted by them in accordance with the Copyright, Designs and Patents Act 1988.

All rights reserved; no part of this publication may be reproduced, stored in a retrieval system, or transmitted in any form or by any means, electronic, mechanical, photocopying, recording, or otherwise without the prior written permission of the Publishers.

First published 2020

ISBN: 978-1-292-33458-5

Set in Mundo Sans
Printed in China (SWTC/01)

**Acknowledgements**
The publishers and author(s) would like to thank the following people and institutions for their feedback and comments during the development of the material: Marcos Mendonça, Leandra Dias, Gisele Aga, Viviane Kirmeliene, Simara H. Dal'Alba, Mônica Bicalho and GB Editorial. The publishers would also like to thank all the teachers who contributed to the development of *Let's learn about...*: Adriano de Paula Souza, Aline Ramos Teixeira Santo, Aline Vitor Rodrigues Pina Pereira, Ana Paula Gomez Montero, Anna Flávia Feitosa Passos, Camila Jarola, Celiane Junker Silva, Edegar França Junior, Fabiana Reis Yoshio, Fernanda de Souza Thomaz, Luana da Silva, Michael Iacovino Luidvinavicius, Munique Dias de Melo, Priscila Rossatti Duval Ferreira Neves, Sandra Ferito, and schools that took part in Construindo Juntos.

**Author Acknowledgements**
Rhiannon S. Ball

**Credit Image(s):**
**BBC Worldwide Learning:** 6, 6, 6, 8, 10, 12, 14, 16, 18, 20, 22, 24, 26, 28, 30, 32, 34, 36, 38, 40, 42, 44, 46, 48, 50, 52, 54, 56, 58, 62, 64, 66, 68, 70
**Pearson Education** Ltd: Silva Serviços de Educação 10, 10, 10, 10, 10, 14, 22, 26, 28, 32, 32, 32, 36, 44, 46, 52, 54, 60, 60, 62, 62, 64, 68, 68, 68
**Shutterstock.com:** BeRad 14, Iryna Dobrovynska 32, Natalia Sheinkin 16, NotionPic 68

**Illustration Acknowledgements**
Illustrated by Filipe Laurentino and Silva Serviços de Educação

**Cover illustration** © Filipe Laurentino

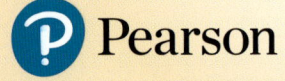

# Contents

| | | |
|---|---|---|
| | Table of contents | 4 |
| | Presentation | 6 |
| U1 | What do you like about yourself? | 8 |
| U2 | Why do we go to school? | 16 |
| U3 | How can you help your family? | 24 |
| U4 | Why do we feel hot or cold? | 32 |
| U5 | What other living things are around us? | 40 |
| U6 | Why is food important? | 48 |
| U7 | How can farm animals help us? | 56 |
| U8 | Who lives and works in my town? | 64 |

# Table of contents - CBeebies

| UNIT | LESSON 1 | LESSON 2 | LESSON 3 | LESSON 4 |
|---|---|---|---|---|
| **Unit 1**<br>**What do you like about yourself?**<br>page 8 | • Identify different kinds of hair and describe their hair<br>• Develop creative and motor skills in context<br>• Understand familiar words in a video | • Practice measuring length<br>• Recognize patterns and distinguish length in context<br>• Use visuals to understand a video | • Reflect on how certain situations make them and others feel.<br>• Develop creative and cognitive skills in context<br>• Explain understanding of a video | • Reflect on how certain situations make them and others feel.<br>• Develop creative and cognitive skills in context<br>• Give their opinion on a video |
| **Unit 2**<br>**Why do we go to school?**<br>page 16 | • Discuss the way our behavior makes others feel<br>• Recognize and identify people as friends<br>• Watch and follow a story in a video | • Understand and use opposite adjectives<br>• Explore different surfaces and how they feel<br>• Use visuals to understand a video | • Understand instructions<br>• Develop creative and cognitive skills in context<br>• Explain understanding of a video | • Understand instructions<br>• Develop creative and cognitive skills in context<br>• Give their opinion on a video |
| **Unit 3**<br>**How can you help your family?**<br>page 24 | • Talk about chores<br>• Develop creative and imaginative skills in context<br>• Explain understanding of a video | • Name household chores and the people who do them<br>• Identify where different things belong in your bedroom<br>• Use visuals to understand a video | • Talk about chores<br>• Develop cognitive skills in context<br>• Use visuals to understand a video | • Talk about chores<br>• Identify different jobs in the house<br>• Give their opinion on a video |
| **Unit 4**<br>**Why do we feel hot or cold?**<br>page 32 | • Make connections between the weather and the clothes we wear<br>• Categorize clothes according to hot and cold weather<br>• Understand familiar words in a video | • Make connections between the weather and the clothes we wear<br>• Express preference in relation to clothes<br>• Use visuals to understand a video | • Practice saying words for clothes<br>• Identify purpose and size differences in context<br>• Use visuals to understand a video | • Understand, observe and record the weather outside<br>• Identify different clouds and their function<br>• Give their opinion on a video |

| UNIT | LESSON 1 | LESSON 2 | LESSON 3 | LESSON 4 |
|---|---|---|---|---|
| **Unit 5**<br>**What other living things are around us?**<br>page 40 | • Learn to recognize and name some of the creatures that live in the garden<br>• Develop creative and motor skills in context<br>• Use visuals to understand a video | • Learn to recognize and name some of the creatures that live in the garden<br>• Develop creative and imaginative skills in context<br>• Give their opinion on a video | • Describe the appearance and behavior of insects<br>• Understand the stages of development of a butterfly<br>• Use visuals to understand a video | • Understand that plants are living things with specific needs and describe its life cycle<br>• Identify the stages of plant growth in context<br>• Give their opinion on a video |
| **Unit 6**<br>**Why is food important?**<br>page 48 | • Talk about food items and healthy food<br>• Identify and recognize vegetables that grow underground and above ground<br>• Give their opinion on a video | • Talk about food items and healthy food<br>• Understand simple plant growth through experiments<br>• Understand an animated video | • Talk about utensils we use to eat<br>• Express preferences in context<br>• Understand familiar words in a video | • Talk about food items<br>• Identify ingredients and processes to make a cake<br>• Watch and follow a story in a video |
| **Unit 7**<br>**How can farm animals help us?**<br>page 56 | • Understand what products animals produce<br>• Develop creative and motor skills in context<br>• Use visuals to understand a video | • Talk about farm animals and the sounds they make<br>• Develop creative and motor skills in context<br>• Understand an animated video | • Talk about woolen clothes and how they are done<br>• Develop creative and motor skills in context<br>• Watch and follow a story in a video | • Understand what products animals produce<br>• • Identify specific animals, their produce and function<br>• Give their opinion on a video |
| **Unit 8**<br>**Who lives and works in my town?**<br>page 64 | • Talk about what construction workers and firefighters use at work<br>• Develop motor skills in context<br>• Use visuals to understand a video | • Talk about what construction workers and firefighters use at work<br>• Understand the role of firefighters<br>• Explain understanding of a video | • Understand how nurses and doctors can help<br>• Recognize common illnesses<br>• Understand an animated video | • Understand how nurses and doctors can help<br>• Identify and make suggestions on how to feel better<br>• Explain understanding of a video |

# Presentation

***Let's Learn About...*** is a bilingual program which aims to develop a wide variety of skills and knowledge of different subjects. To this end, several additional components ensure that students work on creative learning, pre-coding, *STEAM* lessons, personal, social, and emotional development, and much more. Teachers can find a complete mapping of the components online and suggested weekly planning to help them make the most of our interdisciplinary approach. All of the components in the program provide students with the opportunity to build a solid foundation and prepare themselves for the challenges ahead. The lessons help children explore and learn more about the world around them. The CBeebies *Project Book* introduceds videos as a fun, educational tool for the preschool classroom.

## Learning principles behind the CBeebies component

*CBeebies* is a British television channel that is owned by the BBC. It produces and broadcasts content for children aged below six.

Preschool children are considered the digital generation; they do not know a life without screens and technology. Although excessive screen time is not advised for children in this age group, controlled access to quality content can aid students' development. In **Let's Learn About...** screen time is not a passive, individual activity; on the contrary, students are invited to share the watching experience together, with the well-planned interruptions from the teacher to highlight important language and plot developments to speed up students' language acquisition and work on creative and critical thinking skills.

The *CBeebies* videos used in **Let's Learn About...** have been carefully curated by education specialists at the BBC to ensure that they match students' learning needs and developmental abilities. The videos contain episodes of popular *CBeebies* TV shows, including both animated cartoons and documentary-style programs.

Familiarity is important for learning at this age and involving characters in learning material can help with this. In each volume of *CBeebies*, students will watch several episodes of each TV show, helping them grow a love for the characters, which in turn increases motivation and excitement about the lessons.

## How to work with the CBeebies Project Book

All **Let's learn about...** Project Books may have their pages removed. Before starting an activity in their Project Books, students can be instructed to take out the page they are going to work on and add it to a folder of their choice, so that students' work can be shared with parents regularly. This page, together with the projects students have developed in other project lessons, can become part of a portfolio created alongside with the teacher.

The aim of a portfolio is to show the cumulative efforts and progress students have made over time. This is also a great way to evaluate their improvement in all learning areas and the mastery of several skills. Students should be encouraged to share the work in their portfolio with their parents so that they can support their child's learning and be an active part of their development as a student. An assessment chart is available in the Extra Resources folder at Pearson English Portal for teachers to print and fill out with students' performance and attached to the portfolio folder.

**Kit and Pup**

**Sarah and Duck**

**Yakka Dee**

## What's in a CBeebies lesson?

*CBeebies* lessons follow similar routines to the ones that students develop in all the *Let's Learn About...* components, including the visual schedule, attention-getters, and *hello* and *goodbye* songs and routines.

In each lesson, students do a *before watching*, *while watching*, and *after watching* activity related to an episode of a *CBeebies* TV show. The *before watching* activity aims at introducing and practicing key language that will appear in the video; the *while watching* video is the moment when students watch the video with the teacher, during which guidance is given at specific moments to pause the video to ask questions, check students' understanding, etc.; and the *after watching* activity gives students the opportunity to reflect on the video further through a Project Book, craft, or role-play activity.

For each unit, there are two CLIL videos and one story time video; therefore, one video is watched over two lessons, giving students the opportunity to rewatch enjoyable content (something that children in this age group love to do!) and then reflect on it from a different angle. The story time videos feature an episode from the following TV shows: Nelly and Nora (Volume 1) Sarah and Duck (Volume 2), Go Jetters (Volume 3). Before you show these videos, we suggest that you say to students, *We're going to watch another episode of (Nelly and Nora). What is (Nelly) like? And (Nora)? Do you remember what happened in the last episode? What do you think happens today?* You can do this in a mixture of L1 and English or only in L1, according to your students' abilities.

There are two Project Book pages per unit instead of one per lesson, which adds variety to classes and keeps students motivated.

Lessons involve a mixture of games, craft making, singing, and drawing activities, which provide an important contrast to the video time activity, during which students should be reminded to sit still and watch quietly.

## Components

### For teachers
- CBeebies Teacher's Guide
- Video library with *CBeebies* videos available at Pearson English Portal
- Audio library with songs available at Pearson English Portal

### For students
- *CBeebies* Project Book with stickers

## Taking it further

If you notice that your students are developing a love for the characters featured in the *CBeebies* videos, you may like to access the official websites for these shows and download the additional resources, such as coloring pages and craft activities, featuring the characters for students to work on at home or during a rainy-day recess. The *CBeebies* official website also contains additional activities and useful articles.

### CBeebies
https://global.cbeebies.com/
https://global.cbeebies.com/grown-ups/ (for educators and parents)

### Go Jetters
https://www.gojetters.com/

### Sarah and Duck
https://www.sarahandduck.com/

### Yakka Dee
http://yakkadee.com/
[All links accessed on October 22, 2019]

# Unit 1 What do you like about yourself?

**Learning goals**
- Identify different kinds of hair and describe their hair
- Develop creative and motor skills in context
- Understand familiar words in a video

**Main language content**
Colors
Hair: *hair; curly, long, short, straight*
Possessive adjectives: *my, your*

## OPENING

### Circle time

**Materials and preparation**
- Audio library – songs
- Puppet
- Visual schedule pictures

Stand together in a circle and sing the *Hello song* (track 2). Say *hello* to the puppet and ask, *How are you?* Everyone asks each other.
Teach them the attention-getter, *1, 2, 3 It's time for…CBeebies!* Use the attention-getter every time you expect students to listen to you. After that, bring out the visual schedule pictures. Spread them out in the middle of the circle. Ask students to help you select the pictures that show today's schedule as you tell them what they are going to do today.

### Play *In my classroom.*

**Materials and preparation**
- Flashcards: *face, head, eyes, ears, mouth*

Slowly reveal each of the flashcards and elicit the words from students. Then play a quick game to review the words. Stand up together in a circle, pass one flashcard to the student on your right and another flashcard to the student on your left. Continue giving flashcards right and left. Students say the word and pass it on.

## ACTIVE LEARNING

### Before watching the video – My hair type

**Materials and preparation**

- Printourt: *straight hair, curly hair, long hair, short hair*

Sit together in a circle, show each picture in turn and make gestures to show and reinforce the hair types (e.g. mime brushing long/short hair; moving your finger in circular movements to show curly hair, etc.). Go around the circle, encourage students to describe each of their classmates' hair type. Introduce and focus on color, too.

> **Note to teachers**
> Use dolls or puppets with the different hair types if you can. This means students can feel the different hair types, too.

### Watching the video - Let's watch!

**Materials and preparation**

- Video library

Sit together in a semicircle so everyone can see the screen. *Play Yakka Dee, Series 2, Ep1* Hair (Video 1). Watch the video together. Watch it again and stop each time there is a different hair type. Encourage students to call out the hair type and mime using their hands.
You should set expectations of correct watching behavior, reminding students that they should sit still and watch quietly, respecting their classmates.

### After watching the video – Make a craft "puppet."

**Materials and preparation**

- A4 construction paper (cut into circles)
- Curling ribbon
- Glue
- Pencil
- Scissors
- Wool (different colors)
- Wooden spoons (if available)

Sit students at their tables and give each student a large circle of A4 construction paper. Put the wool and curling ribbon in the middle of the table. Students select the "hair" – wool or curling ribbon – they want to stick on the head and glue it on. Students can then draw a face on the head.

> **Note to teachers**
> If possible, you can give each student a wooden spoon to stick on the hair and draw on a face. Then they can role-play conversations between their wooden spoon puppets.

## DIFFERENTIATED INSTRUCTION

### BELOW LEVEL
### After watching the video

Focus on only *long hair* and *short hair* and ask students to create a head and hair based on their own.

### ABOVE LEVEL
### After watching the video

Sit together in a circle with the craft head and hair. Students describe their picture or puppet, e.g. *She has curly hair.* Students then mingle with their craft picture or puppet and compare.

## CLOSING

### Talk about the video. Sing the *Goodbye song.*

**Materials and preparation**

- Audio library – songs

Talk with students about the video. Ask, *What did Yakka Dee talk about? What hair types did they see?*
Play the *Goodbye song* (track 3) and invite students to sing along while they put their things away. Encourage students to help each other and take responsibility for the classroom space. Say *goodbye* to them and have them say *goodbye* back to you.

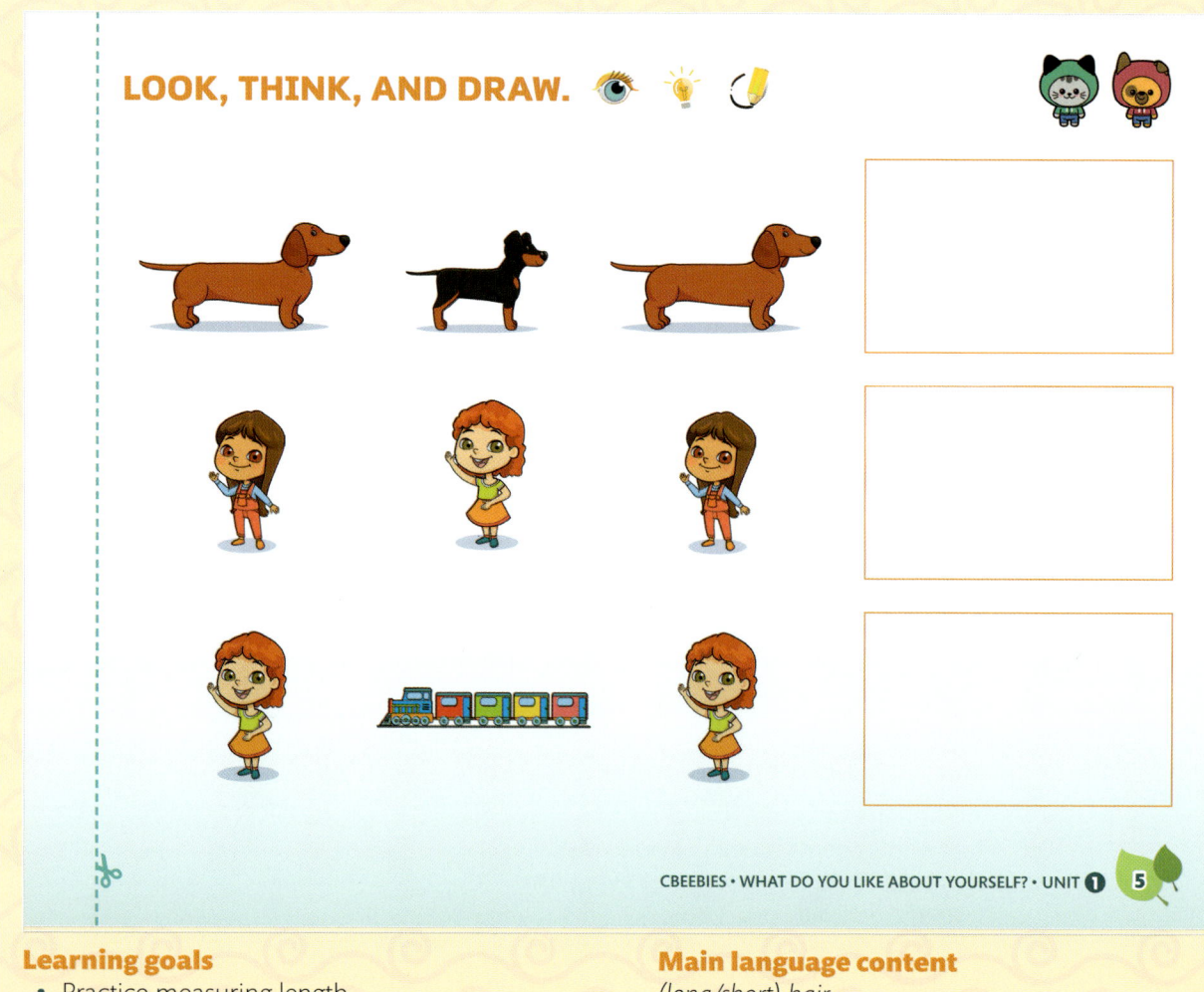

### Learning goals
- Practice measuring length
- Recognize patterns and distinguish length in context
- Use visuals to understand a video

### Main language content
(long/short) hair
It's a (long/short) (dog/slide/train).

# OPENING

### Circle time

**Materials and preparation**
- Puppet
- Days of the week poster
- Weather flashcards

Stand together in a circle and sing the *Hello song* (track 2). Say *hello* to the puppet and ask, *How are you?* Everyone asks each other. Talk to students about the visual schedule, showing them the pictures as you say the activities they are going to do. Have the class helper of the day order the pictures of the activities as they are mentioned.

> **Note to teachers**
> Listen to what your students want to say and take notes so you can begin to feed in the English to them.

### Hair types

**Materials and preparation**
- Printouts: *long hair, short hair, curly hair, straight hair*

Sit together in a circle and reveal each of the hair types flashcards by flashing the printout quickly. Encourage students to call out the words. Stick the printouts up around the room, stand with students in the middle, and make gestures related to a hair type (e.g. brushing a long/short hair; moving your finger in circular movements to mime curly hair, etc.). Students run to the correct printout. Take away the printouts from the walls, make gestures related to a hair type, and invite students to say the words (e.g. long, curly, short, etc.
You should set expectations of walking safely so as to avoid accidents.

## ACTIVE LEARNING

### Before watching the video – Long or short?

### Materials and preparation
- Building blocks
- Printouts: long train, short train, long slide, short slide, long dog, short dog, bricks

Sit together in a circle. Make a short line and a long line using the blocks. Focus on the *long* and *short* distinction. Show students the printouts and invite them to tell you if the items are long or short. Mix up all the flashcards and invite students to sort them into *long* and *short* items.

> **Note to teachers**
> Invite students to find other examples in the classroom or in the playground – for example, *pencils, rulers, sticks*, etc.

### Watching the video Let's watch!

### Materials and preparation
- Video library

Sit together in a semicircle so everyone can see the screen. Play *Kit & Pup*, Series 1, Ep 12, *Long and Short* (Video 2). Watch the video together. Watch it again and stop at each long and short item. Ask students what they can see and show you if it's long or short.

You should set expectations of correct watching behavior, reminding students that they should sit still and watch quietly, respecting their classmates.

### After watching the video – Look, think, and draw.

### Materials and preparation
- Colored pencils
- Project Book page 5
- Pencils

Sit students at their tables. Help them open their Project Books to page 5. Point to the pictures and say the next picture in the sequence together. Give students a pencil each and tell them to draw the picture to complete the sequence.

> **Note to teachers**
> Fast finishers can color the pictures. Encourage students to say the words as they draw.

## DIFFERENTIATED INSTRUCTION

### BELOW LEVEL
### Before watching the video
Focus on only the blocks to show *short* and *long*. Get a set for small groups, call out *a short line* or *a long line* and students put together the lines.

### ABOVE LEVEL
### Before watching the video
Invite students to draw more items that are long and short and tell you about them, using their previous language knowledge (for example, *long neck, short neck; long nose, short nose*).

## CLOSING

### Make a long train. Sing the *Goodbye song*.

### Materials and preparation
- Audio library – songs
- Building blocks

Sit in a circle with students. Make a "train" with the blocks. Tell students that you want to make the train long, and invite a student to help you. They can add blocks. Then repeat with *short* and invite students to take away blocks. Continue in this way, asking students to make the train of blocks longer or shorter. Make sure different students participate.
Sing the *Goodbye song* (track 3) and invite students to sing along while they put their things away. Encourage students to help each other and take responsibility for the classroom space. Say *goodbye* to them and have them say *goodbye* back to you.

**Learning goals**
- Reflect on how certain situations make them and others feel.
- Develop creative and motor skills in context

**Video objective**
- Explain understanding of a video

**Main language content**
Animals: *donkey, duck*
Food: *carrot*
*Why are you (happy/sad)?*
*What makes you happy?*

# OPENING

## Circle time

**Materials and preparation**
- Audio library – songs
- Puppet

Stand together in a circle and sing the *Hello song* (track 2). Say *hello* to the puppet and ask, *How are you?* Everyone asks each other.
Review the attention-getter, *1, 2, 3 It's time for... CBeebies!*
Talk to students about the visual schedule, showing them the pictures as you say the activities they are going to do. Have the class helper of the day order the pictures of the activities as they are mentioned.

> **Note to teachers**
> Remind students that they should be quiet and look at you when they hear the attention-getter.

## Sing *If you're happy and you know it.*

**Materials and preparation**
- Audio library – songs

Stand together in a circle. Sing *If you're happy and you know it* (track 7) together and do the actions. Repeat the song several times to give students a chance to practice the language. Pause after "*...and you know it*" and encourage students to say, *clap your hands* and do the action.

CBeebies

# ACTIVE LEARNING

### Before watching the video – Donkey and duck

### Materials and preparation
- Drawing of a happy and a sad face
- Plastic or real carrot (optional)
- Printouts or stuffed animals: donkey, duck

Sit together in a circle. Show students the printouts/stuffed animals. Ask, *What animal is this?* Elicit or teach *donkey* and *duck*. Talk to students about these animals, e.g. where they can see them, what they know about them, etc. Show the drawings of the happy and sad faces and elicit *happy* and *sad*. Place the happy face next to the donkey and ask, *What makes a donkey happy?* Repeat with *sad*. Then repeat with the duck. Encourage all students to participate.

> **Note to teachers**
> Get students ready for the video by showing a plastic or a real carrot and asking students if carrots make them happy. Ask, *Why (not)?*

### Watching the video - Let's watch!

### Materials and preparation
- Video library

Sit together in a semicircle so everyone can see the screen. Play *Sarah and Duck, Ep 3, Cheer up Donkey* (Video 3). Watch the video together. Watch the video again and stop when you see the duck and donkey. Ask, *What makes you happy?* At the end ask students what makes the donkey happy.

You should set expectations of correct watching behavior, reminding students that they should sit still and watch quietly, respecting their classmates.

### After watching the video – Donkey craft

### Materials and preparation
- Colored markers
- Glue
- Scissors
- Sheets of gray and orange construction paper cutout into circles and ear shapes (gray) and carrots (orange)

Have students at their tables and put the craft materials in the middle of the table. Give students the circles of construction paper. Tell students it's the donkey's face. Ask students about donkey ears and cut out two big ears from the construction paper. Show students how to stick on the ears. Tell students the donkey is happy. Give them a carrot cutout to stick in the donkey's mouth.

# DIFFERENTIATED INSTRUCTION

### BELOW LEVEL
### Before watching the video
Show students only the donkey and carrot pictures. Tell students carrots make donkeys happy. Together with students, mime being sad donkeys with no carrot and then happy donkeys.

### ABOVE LEVEL
### After watching the video
Once students have finished, invite students to mingle around the class with their donkey craft, asking and answering about what makes them happy.

# CLOSING

### Play *Duck, Duck, Donkey*. Say goodbye.

Sit students in a circle to play a variation of the classic game, *Duck, Duck, Goose*, changing *goose* to *donkey*. One student stands up and walks around the circle, touching each classmate on the head and saying, *duck*. At any moment they choose, they can switch and say, *donkey*. The student who is touched as they hear *donkey* stands up and chases the other student around the circle. The student who was touching heads tries to sit in the other student's place in the circle before being caught. It is now the other student's turn to walk around the circle. Play a few rounds and then say *goodbye* to students. Have them say *goodbye* to you, too.

**Learning goals**
- Reflect on how certain situations make them and others feel
- Develop cognitive and creative skills in context
- Give their opinion on a video

**Main language content**
Animals: *donkey, duck*
Food: *bread, carrot*
*Why are you (happy/sad)?*
*What makes you happy?*

# OPENING

### Circle time

**Materials and preparation**
- Audio library – songs
- Puppet
- Visual schedule pictures

Stand together in a circle and sing the *Hello song* (track 2). Say *hello* to the puppet and ask, *How are you?* Everyone asks each other.
Talk to students about the visual schedule, showing them the pictures as you say the activities they are going to do. Have the class helper of the day order the pictures of the activities as they are mentioned.

### Happy and sad music

**Materials and preparation**
- A selection of sound effects or clips of happy and sad music (these can easily be found on the Internet)

Stand together in a circle. Play the sound effects/clips one by one. After each one ask, *How does it make you feel? Happy or sad?* Encourage all students to share their ideas and give reasons.

> **Note to teachers**
> You can extend this activity by asking students to do a happy or a sad dance for each sound effect/music clip.

14 CBeebies

# ACTIVE LEARNING

### Before watching the video – Duck and donkey

### Materials and preparation
- A toy duck and donkey
- Audio library – songs

Show students the toys and practice the words *duck* and *donkey*. Ask students, *Where can you see a duck? And a donkey?* Talk to them about each animal. Then play a song from the Audio library and have students move around the room like a duck or a donkey. Change the animal occasionally; students have to listen carefully to you and change animals.

> **Note to teachers**
> Organize the class into two groups (ducks and donkeys), and students mime being each animal and being sad and happy.

### Watching the video
### Materials and preparation
- Video library

Sit together in a semicircle so everyone can see the screen. Play *Sarah and Duck, Ep 3, Cheer up Donkey* (Video 3). Watch the video together. Watch the video again and ask what makes donkey happy and what doesn't make donkey happy. Stop and ask where Sarah, Duck, and Donkey visit in the video.

### After watching the video – Look, think, and draw.
### Materials and preparation
- Colored pencils
- Project Book page 7

Sit students at their tables. Help them open their Project Books to page 7. Point to the pictures and ask, *What is this?* Encourage them to say *donkey, duck*. Put the colored markers in the middle of the table. Invite students to draw what makes each animal happy in the box under the pictures of donkey and duck. Encourage them to draw the things they see in the video (carrot and bread) and then use their imagination to draw other things. Then in the third box they draw what makes them feel happy.

> **Note to teachers**
> To support students with ideas, draw a few examples of things that can make you happy on the board.

# DIFFERENTIATED INSTRUCTION

### BELOW LEVEL
### After watching the video
### Materials and preparation
- Pictures of things that make students happy, e.g. ice cream, toys, etc.

Show the pictures and ask students if the items make them happy. Stick the pictures that make students happy on the board for students to copy into the Project Book.

### Above level
### After watching the video

Encourage students to think about the animals' needs and how these things make them happy, for example the environment they need to be comfortable, the weather conditions they prefer, who they like to be with, etc.

# CLOSING

### Show and tell. Sing the *Goodbye song*.
### Materials and preparation
- Audio library – songs
- Project Book page 7

Organize students into pairs or small groups. Students sit together with their Project Books to show, share, and tell each other what makes them happy.
Sing the *Goodbye song* (track 3) and invite students to sing along. Say *goodbye* to them and have them say *goodbye* back to you.

# Unit 2 Why do we go to school?

**Learning goals**
- Discuss the way their behavior makes others feel
- Recognize and identify people as friends
- Watch and follow a story in a video

**Main language content**
Fun: *hug, smile, tickle*
People: *friends*
*I'm your friend. You're my friend. We're friends.*

## OPENING

### Circle time

**Materials and preparation**
- Audio library – songs
- Puppet
- Visual schedule pictures

Stand together in a circle and sing the *Hello song* (track 2). Say *hello* to the puppet and ask, *How are you?*
Teach the attention-getter *Everybody look at me, it's time for CBeebies!* Remind students that they should be quiet and pay attention whenever you say this.
Show the visual schedule pictures and invite the class helper to help you pick out the ones that represent what you will do today.

> **Note to teachers**
> Review the other attention-getters with students.

### Sing *Everybody do this.*

**Materials and preparation**
- Audio library – songs

Stand together in a circle and sing *Everybody do this* (track 8). Sing it once while acting out smiling, then repeat with tickling, and finally with hugging. Encourage students to sing along and act out each time.

# ACTIVE LEARNING

### Before watching the video – We're friends!

#### Materials and preparation
- Hand puppets (at least three)
- A puppet theater frame (this can just be a large piece of cardboard cut out cinto a frame)

Sit students in a semicircle with the puppet theater frame at the front. Introduce two hand puppet characters and act out a conversation to show their friendship. For example, you could have them greet each other warmly, laugh and joke with each other, hug each other, etc. Introduce another hand puppet and show their friendship. Have the puppets say, *We're friends* and *I'm your friend*; then have them act out *tickle, smile,* and *hug*.

> **Note to teachers**
> Invite students to act out or role-play the actions together. Students smile, hug, and tickle.

### Watching the video – Let's watch!

#### Materials and preparation
- Video library

Sit together in a semicircle so everyone can see the screen. *Play Show Me Show Me, Series 4, Ep 8 Jigsaw & Friends* (Video 4). Watch the video together. Watch it again and act out the actions together.

You should set expectations of correct watching behavior, reminding students that they should sit still and watch quietly, respecting their classmates.

### After watching the video – Look, think, and draw.

#### Materials and preparation
- Colored paints or pencils
- Crayons
- Pencils
- Project Book page 9

Sit students at the table. Help them open their Project Books to page 9. Point to the special frame and tell students they are going to draw their friends in it. Put the colored paints, crayons, and pencils in the middle of the table and allow students to select what they want to use. Students draw or paint their friends.

> **Note to teachers**
> Draw or paint your friends and show the frame to the class, giving some details. Allow students to draw or paint their family if they can't think of friends.

# DIFFERENTIATED INSTRUCTION

### BELOW LEVEL
### After watching the video
Students can just draw and paint their best friend, or a sibling or cousin, rather than trying to draw a lot of different people.

### ABOVE LEVEL
### After watching the video
Encourage students to paint themselves doing what they like to do best with their friends, e.g. playing, dancing, etc. They can add details such as background, toys, etc.

# CLOSING

### Talk about friends. Sing the *Goodbye song*.

#### Materials and preparation
- Audio library – songs

Sit with students in a circle. Invite students one by one to present their picture to the class and explain who it is and what they like the most about their friend(s).

> **Note to teachers**
> If you have a very large group, students can be organized into smaller groups to present their pictures.

Sing the *Goodbye song* (track 3) together. Say *goodbye* to students and have them say *goodbye* back to you.

### Learning goals
- Understand and use opposite adjectives
- Explore different surfaces and how they feel

### Video objective
- Use visuals to understand a video

### Main language content
Adjectives: *rough, smooth*
Nouns: *banana, bark, chair, pineapple, sponge, wood*
*It's (rough). / It feels (smooth).*

# OPENING

### Circle time

#### Materials and preparation
- Audio library – songs
- Puppet
- Days of the week chart

Sit together in a circle and sing the *Hello song* (track 2). Say *hello* to the puppet and ask, *How are you?* Everyone asks each other. Ask students what day it is and use the Days of the week chart. Review the attention-getter, *Everybody look at me, it's time for CBeebies!* and remind students that they need to be quiet and look at you when you say this.

> **Note to teachers**
> Ask students about their weekly routines and what they do on certain days of the week.

### Feely bag

#### Materials and preparation
- Bag or pillowcase
- Ball of yarn
- Brick (a small one, or fragments – made sure these aren't sharp)
- Scrunched up paper
- Soft ball
- Soft toy
- Wooden block

Put all the items in the bag or pillowcase. Sit together in a circle. Ask students what they think is in the bag. Pass the bag around for students to feel from the outside only and tell you what they can feel. Put your hand in the bag and describe what you can feel. Invite students to do the same. Pull out the items to show and say what they feel like.

# ACTIVE LEARNING

## Before watching the video

### Materials and preparation
- A banana
- A piece of bark
- A piece of sponge
- A pineapple

Sit together in a circle and put the items in the middle of of the circle. Pick up a smooth item, feel it, and say *smooth*. Pass it around for students to feel and say the word. Repeat with a rough item. Invite students to pick up and feel other items, and tell you if they are rough or smooth. Invite students to categorize the items into rough and smooth items.

> **Note to teachers**
> Invite students to look at their things, their bag, pencil case, clothing and tell each other if they're rough or smooth.

## Watching the video - Let's watch!

### Materials and preparation
- Video library

Sit together in a circle so everyone can see the screen. Play *Kit & Pup, Series 1, Ep3, Rough & smooth* (Video 5). Watch the video together. Watch it again and stop it every time a rough or smooth item is shown. Invite students to tell you what it is and how it feels.

You should set expectations of correct watching behavior, reminding students that they should sit still and watch quietly, respecting their classmates.

## After watching the video – Rough and smooth mini-book

### Materials and preparation
- Cardboard
- Construction paper (one sheet per student)
- Crepe paper
- Felt
- Glitter
- Glue
- Ribbon
- Sandpaper

Sit students at their tables and give each student a sheet of construction paper. Help them fold the paper in two to make a mini-book. Put the different materials in the middle of the tables and tell students to find and stick something rough on the first page. Repeat with a piece of smooth material on the next page. On the other page students make a collage mixed up of rough-and smooth- feeling materials.

> **Note to teachers**
> If you have time before the class, cut the paper into eight pieces and staple them together so that each student can make a longer book.

# DIFFERENTIATED INSTRUCTION

## BELOW LEVEL
### Before watching the video

### Materials and preparation
- Glue
- Pieces of smooth and rough materials (one piece of each per student)
- Popsicle sticks (one per student)
- Scissors
- Small cards (one per student; optional)

Use only one smooth and a rough piece of material, e.g a sheet of sandpaper and a sheet of Canson paper. Get students to stick those on to a popsicle stick (or on a card) and practice feeling, saying, and noticing the difference.

## ABOVE LEVEL
### After watching the video

In their mini-books, invite students to add an extra page and draw a related object that has a rough and a smooth surface. Help them glue an extra page or staple it to their mini-books. When they finish, students work together in small groups comparing the objects they selected and drew.

# CLOSING

**Play *Jump rope*. Sing the *Goodbye song*.**

### Materials and preparation
- A jump rope
- A selection of rough and smooth material
- Audio library – songs

Take students outside or make space in the classroom. Play the jump rope in the center of the space, and tell students that one side is *smooth* and one side is *rough*. Show the materials one by one. Students jump over to the correct side of the rope according to whether they think its rough or smooth. You should set expectations of moving safely.

Play the *Goodbye song* (track 3) and invite students to sing along while they put their things away. Encourage students to help each other and take responsibility for the classroom space. Say *goodbye* to them and have them say *goodbye* back to you.

**Learning goals**
- Understand instructions
- Develop creative and cognitive skills in context
- Explain understanding of a video

**Main language content**
Adjective: *new*
Nouns: *auto cat, robot, toy*
*Let's build (a robot).*

# OPENING

### Circle time

### Materials and preparation
- Audio library – songs
- Puppet
- Visual schedule pictures

Stand together in a circle and sing the *hello* song (track 2). Say *hello* to the puppet and ask, *How are you?* Everyone asks each other.
Review the attention-getter, *1, 2, 3 It's time for... CBeebies* and remind students what they should do when you say these. Show the visual schedule pictures and ask the class helper to choose the ones that represent what they are going to do today.

> **Note to teachers**
> Review the other attention-getters that students have learned.

### Play *Robot statues.*

### Materials and preparation
- Printout of a robot or a robot toy

Show students the printout or toy of a robot and practice saying the word *robot*. Mime being robots. Then play *Robot statues*. Students move around the class miming being robots. When you call out *statues* they freeze on the spot without moving or wobbling. You should set expectations of moving safely.

CBeebies

## ACTIVE LEARNING

### Before watching the video – Make a robot.

### Materials and preparation
- Building blocks (several per group of students to build a small robot)
- Printout of a robot or a robot toy

Sit together in a circle. Show students the robot. Organize the class into several small groups and give each group some building blocks. Invite students to use the building blocks to make a robot. When they have finished, they can show their robots to their classmates. Encourage them to describe it using colors, and *big/small*, etc.

> **Note to teachers**
> Encourage students to compare the robots, e.g. which is the biggest? Which one is the most colorful, etc?

### Watching the video - Let's watch!

### Materials and preparation
- Video library

Sit in a semicircle and make sure every student can see the screen. Play *Sarah and Duck Series 3, Ep 10, Auto Cat* (Video 6). Watch the video together. Watch the video again and stop to ask what Auto cat needs from Sarah. Stop and ask what Duck wants to build and why Duck is sad.
You should set expectations of correct watching behavior, reminding students that they should sit still and watch quietly, respecting their classmates.

### After watching the video – Make your auto cat.

### Materials and preparation
- Cardboard boxes (various sizes; several boxes to make an auto cat in groups)
- Crepe paper
- Glitter
- Glue
- Paints
- Ribbon
- Scissors
- Video library

Play the video again and pause it so that the image freezes with Auto cat on the screen. Organize students into groups and sit them at their tables. Put the craft resources in the middle of the table. Invite students to make an auto cat robot using the cardboard boxes and use all the craft resources to paint and decorate their auto cat. Monitor and help as needed.

## DIFFERENTIATED INSTRUCTION

### BELOW LEVEL
### Before watching the video

If students struggle to work effectively in groups, work together as a whole class to create one robot using the building blocks.

### ABOVE LEVEL
### Before watching the video

### Materials and preparation
- Crayons

Ask students to add function buttons and explain what they do.

## CLOSING

### Play with your auto cat. Sing the *Goodbye song*.

### Materials and preparation
- Audio library – songs
- Students' auto cat models

Invite students to sit together with their auto cat craft models and play together, making requests as in the video.
Sing the *Goodbye song* (track 3) and invite students to sing along. Say *goodbye* to them and have them say *goodbye* back to you.

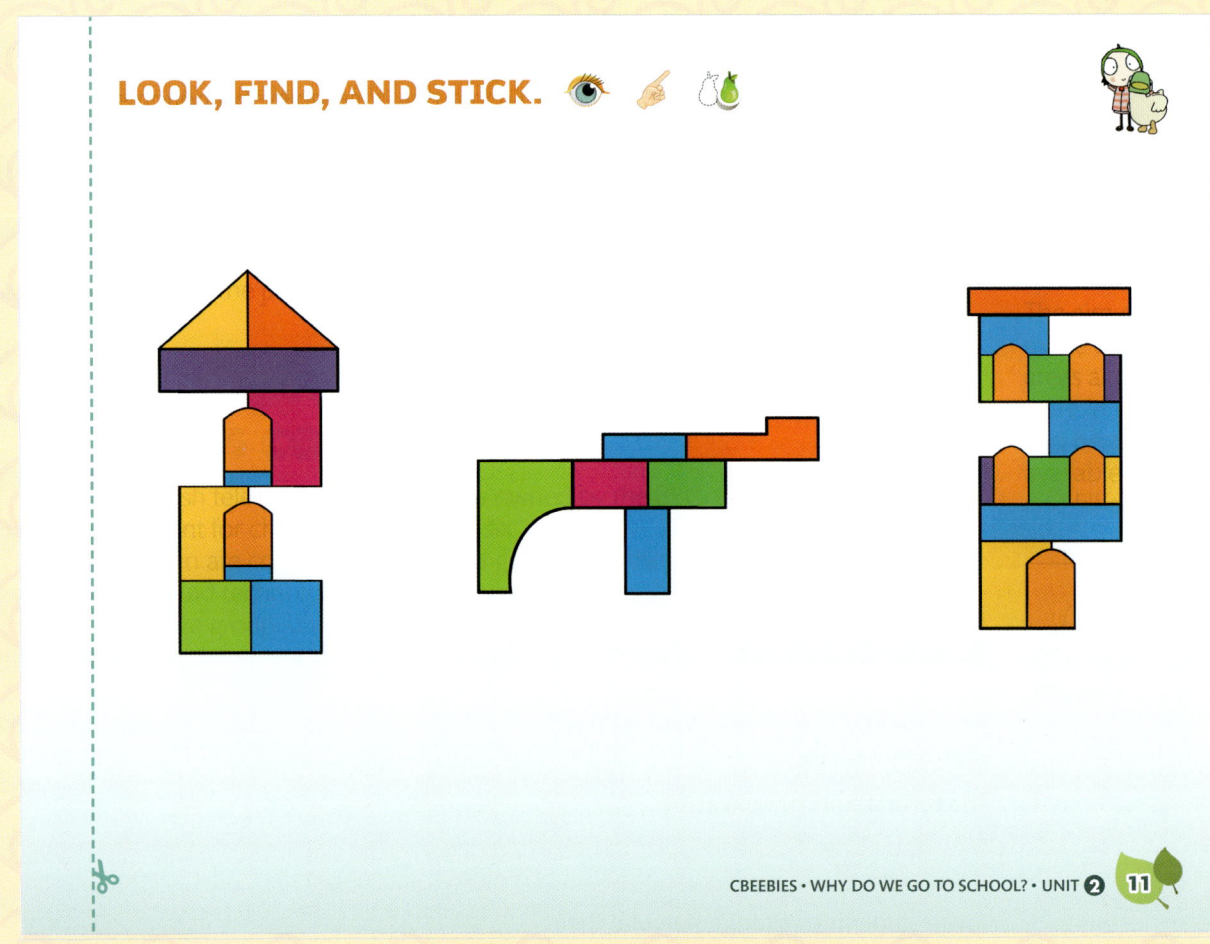

**Learning goals**
- Understand instructions
- Develop cognitive and fine motor skills in context
- Give their opinion on a video

**Main language content**
Adjective: *new*
Nouns: *auto cat, robot, toy*
*Let's build (a robot).*

# OPENING

### Circle time

**Materials and preparation**
- Audio library – songs
- Puppet
- Visual schedule pictures

Stand together in a circle and sing the *hello* song (track 2). Say *hello* to the puppet and ask, *How are you?* Everyone asks each other. Review the attention-getter, *1, 2, 3 It's time for… CBeebies* and remind students what they should do when you say this. Show the visual schedule pictures and ask the class helper to choose the ones that represent what they are going to do today.

> **Note to teachers**
> Review the other attention-getters that students have learned.

### Robot races

**Materials and preparation**
- Balloons (blow up the balloons before class)

Line the students up in two lines. The first two students in the lines put a balloon between their knees and race across the room, acting like a robot, without dropping the balloon. Switch to the next two students in line and continue until every student has raced. You should set expectations of moving safely so as to avoid accidents.

# ACTIVE LEARNING

### Before watching the video – Auto cat

Sit together in a circle. Talk with students about the video from the last class *(Sarah and Duck Series 3, Ep 10, Auto Cat, Video 6)* Ask them if they remember who Auto cat is and what they remember from the video.
Organize students into groups of three and students work together to roleplay the story from the video.

**Note to teachers**

To support students in their role-play, model the main part of the story together as a whole class first.

### Watching the video – Let's watch!
- Video library

Sit together in a semicircle and make sure every student can see the screen. Play *Sarah and Duck Series 3, Ep 10, Auto Duck* (Video 6). Watch the video together. Watch the video again and stop to ask students what the Auto cat needs from Sarah and what Duck wants to build. Ask students what the vet tells Sarah.
You should set expectations of correct watching behavior, reminding students that they should sit still and watch quietly, respecting their classmates.

### After watching the video – Look, find, and stick.

#### Materials and preparation
- Crayons (optional)
- Project Book page 11

Sit students at their tables. Help students open their Project Books to page 11 and invite them to say what they can see. Help students turn to the stickers page and invite them to complete the buildings using the stickers. Help students with the stickers as needed.

## DIFFERENTIATED INSTRUCTION

### BELOW LEVEL
**After watching the video**

Support students by selecting each building block sticker together and finding the corresponding space on page 11.

### ABOVE LEVEL
**After watching the video**

To extend student's language, encourage them to describe the size and color of each building block sticker and where it is placed in the building on the Project Book page.

## CLOSING

### Talk about the videos. Sing the *Goodbye song*.

#### Materials and preparation
- Audio library – songs

Talk with students about the three videos they watched in the unit. Encourage them to recall/act out what they saw in each video and say which was their favorite. Sing the *Goodbye song* (track 3) and invite students to sing along. Say *goodbye* to them and have them say *goodbye* back to you.

# Unit 3 How can you help your family?

**Learning goals**
- Talk about chores
- Develop creative and imaginative skills in context
- Explain understanding of a video

**Main language content**
Adjective: *squashy*
Clean up: *soak up liquid, sponge*
House: *bathroom, kitchen*

## OPENING

**Circle time**

**Materials and preparation**
- Audio library – songs
- Puppet
- Visual schedule pictures

Stand together in a circle and sing the *Hello song* (track 2). Say *hello* to the puppet and ask, *How are you?*
Remind students of the attention-getter, *Everybody look at me, it's time for CBeebies!* Remind students that they should be quiet and pay attention whenever you say this.
Show the visual schedule pictures and invite the class helper to help you pick out the ones that represent what you will do today.

> **Note to teachers**
> Introduce high fives, handshakes, and hugs and allow students to select which greeting they want to receive.

**Play *Musical chairs*.**

**Materials and preparation**
- Audio library – songs

Play *Musical chairs*. Put students' chairs in a big circle facing outward. Play music and students walk around the chairs. Stop the music and students sit down. Take away a chair. Play the music, then stop the music again. Students have to find a chair to sit on. The student that is left without a chair has to sit out. Continue until there is only one student and one chair left. You should set expectations of walking safely so as to avoid accidents.

> **Note to teachers**
> Keep the other students who are out of the game occupied by encouraging them to shout out words of encouragement to their classmates, etc.

# ACTIVE LEARNING

### Before watching the video – Sponges

### Materials and preparation

- 4 sponges
- Printouts: bathroom, kitchen, garage with a car

Sit together in a circle and show students a real sponge. Pass it around the circle for students to look at and feel the sponge. Explain that sponges are squishy and have little holes. Ask students what we do with sponges. Show each printout and say the name of the room in the house. Ask, *How can we use the sponge here?* Students look and mime using the sponge in each situation.

> **Note to teachers**
> Encourage students to use their imagination to come up with other uses for sponges (for example, as a pillow or ear plug).

### Watching the video - Let's watch!

### Materials and preparation

- Video library

Sit together in a semicircle so everyone can see the screen. Play *Kit & Pup, Series 1, Ep 36 Sponge* (Video 7). Watch the video together. Watch it again and stop to check understanding of what sponges can do and where you can see sponges. Invite students to mime using a sponge in different situations.

You should set expectations of correct watching behavior, reminding students that they should sit still and watch quietly, respecting their classmates.

### After watching the video – Sponge free-painting

### Materials and preparation

- A4 construction paper
- Aprons (one per student)
- Watercolor paints
- Sponges (different colors and size; several for each group of students)

Give each student an apron and tell/help them put it on. Remind them that aprons help to keep our clothes clean. Sit students at their tables and give each student a sheet of A4 construction paper. Put the watercolor paints in the middle of the table and lots of different sponges. Invite students to experiment with the sponges to create a painting. Help students write their names on their pictures when they have finished.

> **Note to teachers**
> This is a good opportunity for students to explore patterns independently and see how sponges absorb liquid.

# DIFFERENTIATED INSTRUCTION

### BELOW LEVEL
### After watching the video

Work with only one color and one size and type of sponge to allow students to focus on the task.

### ABOVE LEVEL
### After watching the video

Invite students to try and create specific things with their sponges, for example, an elephant or a car.

# CLOSING

### Art gallery. Sing the *Goodbye song*.

### Materials and preparation

- Audio library – songs

Display students' pictures around the classroom. Encourage them to walk around looking at their classmates' pictures. Then have students sit in a circle and say which painting(s) they liked best.
Sing the *Goodbye song* (track 3) and invite students to sing along. Say *goodbye* to them and have them say *goodbye* back to you.

**Learning goals**
- Name household chores and the people who do them
- Identify where different things belong in their bedroom
- Use visuals to understand a video

**Main language content**
Chores: *clean up, put away (your/our) things, sweep, vacuum*
*It's messy/a mess.*
*Let's (clean up).*

# OPENING

### Circle time

**Materials and preparation**
- Audio library – songs
- Puppet
- Visual schedule pictures

Stand together in a circle and sing the *Hello song* (track 2). Say *hello* to the puppet and ask, *How are you?* Everyone asks each other. Remind students of the attention-getter, *Everybody look at me, it's time for CBeebies!* Remind students that they should be quiet and pay attention whenever you say this.
Show the visual schedule pictures and invite the class helper to help you pick out the ones that represent what you will do today.

> **Note to teachers**
> Remind students of the other attention-getters that they know.

### Organize the classroom.

**Materials and preparation**
- Classroom objects

Sit together in a circle. Take an item from each area of the classroom; for example, a book from the reading corner, toys from the play corner, crayons from the stationary corner, and place them in the middle of the circle. Invite students to look, find, and put away each item.

# ACTIVE LEARNING

### Before watching the video – Where do we put it?

### Materials and preparation
- Printouts: book, bookshelf, toy box, toys, T-shirt, wardrobe

Sit together in a circle and slowly reveal each picture. Mix all the printouts up face down and call out an item for students to find. Stick the *wardrobe*, *toy box*, and *bookshelf* printouts on the board and leave the other printouts mixed up. Invite students to organize by matching up the printouts on the floor with the printouts on the board.

> **Note to teachers**
> Introduce the rhyme from the video clip and sing it together, *Tidying it up, getting it done, so it looks nice for everyone.*

### Watching the video.

### Materials and preparation
- Video library

Sit together in a semicircle so everyone can see the screen. Play *Show Me Show Me*, Series 4, Ep 16, Orangutans & Tidying up (Video 8). Watch the video together. Watch it again and stop to mime tidying and doing the actions of sweeping and vacuuming. Say the rhyme together.

You should set expectations of correct watching behavior, reminding students that they should sit still and watch quietly, respecting their classmates.

### After watching the video – Look, think, and stick.

### Materials and preparation
- Project Book page 13

Sit students at their tables. Help them open their Project Books to page 13 and say what they can see. Help them turn to the stickers page at the back of the Project Books. Elicit what the stickers show and ask them where they would put these objects in their bedroom. Students turn back to page 13, look and decide where to stick the stickers. They stick them in the correct place in the bedroom. Help them with the stickers as needed.

# DIFFERENTIATED INSTRUCTION

### BELOW LEVEL
### Before watching the video
Introduce only the *toy* and *toybox* pictures. Invite students to tidy up the play area in class while playing and singing the tidy-up rhyme from the video, (*Tidying it up, getting it done, so it looks nice for everyone*).

### ABOVE LEVEL
### Before watching the video
Invite students to tell you more items that live in a wardrobe or a toy box and ask what books are on the shelf in their bedroom.

# CLOSING

### Clean up, Sing the *Goodbye song.*

### Materials and preparation
- Audio library – songs
- Video library

Play the tidy-up rhyme from the video and invite students to sing along while they put their things away. Encourage students to say the places in class where items are kept. Sing the *Goodbye song* (track 3) and invite students to sing along. Say *goodbye* to them and have them say *goodbye* back to you.

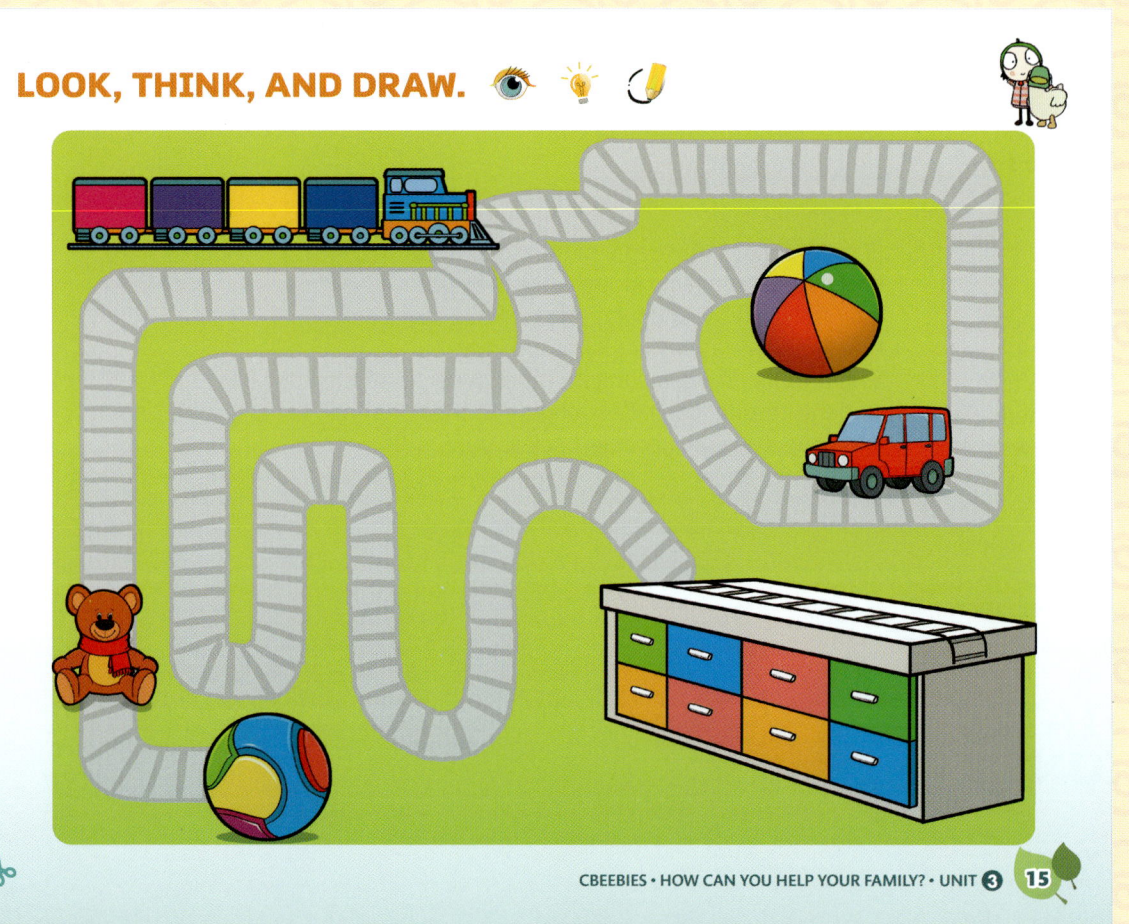

## OPENING

### Circle time

**Materials and preparation**
- Audio library – songs
- Puppet
- Visual schedule pictures

Stand together in a circle and sing the *Hello song* (track 2). Say *hello* to the puppet and ask, *How are you?*
Remind students of the attention-getter, *Everybody look at me, it's time for CBeebies!* Remind students that they should be quiet and pay attention whenever you say this.
Show the visual schedule pictures and invite the class helper to help you pick out the ones that represent what you will do today.

> **Note to teachers**
> Review the other attention-getters that students have learned.

### Mirror, mirror
Stand students in two lines, A and B, opposite each other. Line A will make any movement they like, and line B must be a mirror, copying each movement exactly. Then have students switch roles.

**Learning goals**
- Talk about chores
- Develop cognitive skills in context
- Use visuals to understand a video

**Main language content**
Toys
*It's messy/untidy.*
*Ready to tidy?*
*We need to tidy.*

## ACTIVE LEARNING

### Before watching the video – Let's tidy up!

**Materials and preparation**

- A printout of a picture of a messy bedroom
- Before the class, disorganize each area of the classroom a little

Sit together in a circle. Show students the picture of the messy bedroom. Ask students what they can see and what the problem is. Ask, *How can we tidy it up?* Encourage students to share their ideas. Organize students into groups and assign each group an area of the classroom to tidy up and put things in the correct place.

> **Note to teachers**
> Introduce and encourage students to say, *We need to tidy* and *Ready to tidy?*

### Watching the video – Let's watch!

**Materials and preparation**

- Video library

Sit together in a semicircle and make sure every student can see the screen. Play *Sarah and Duck Series 2, Ep 13, Toy Tidy* (Video 9). Watch the video together. Watch the video again and stop to ask student what toys they can see and where the toys are. Ask students what solution Sarah and Duck use to tidy up.
You should set expectations of correct watching behavior, reminding students that they should sit still and watch quietly, respecting their classmates.

### After watching the video – Look, think, and draw.

**Materials and preparation**

- Colored pencils
- Pencils
- Project Book page 15

Sit students at their tables. Help students open their Project Books to page 13. Point to the train and the drawers, and say that they need to find the path that the train needs to take to get to the drawers. Students find the path by tracing with their fingers, and then draw the line with their pencils. When they finish they can draw and color trains in the train carriages.

> **DIFFERENTIATED INSTRUCTION**
>
> **BELOW LEVEL**
> **After watching the video**
> To support students, draw a train on the board and draw the beginning of the train tracks. Invite students to come to the board and draw tracks.
>
> **ABOVE LEVEL**
> **After watching the video**
> Once students have finished, invite students to sit together and say what is blocking the other train tracks.

## CLOSING

### Clean up. Sing the *Goodbye song*.

**Materials and preparation**

- Audio library – songs

Clean up together and encourage students to help each other and take responsibility for the classroom environment. Encourage them to sing the rhyme from the video as they do so.
Sing the *Goodbye song* (track 3) and invite students to sing along. Say *goodbye* to them and have them say *goodbye* back to you.

Unit 3

**Learning goals**
- Talk about chores
- Identify different jobs in the house
- Give their opinion on a video

**Main language content**
Chores: *put away your clothes, tidy up, wash-up*
*Ready to tidy?*
*We need to (tidy up).*
*What are we going to do?*

# OPENING

### Circle time

### Materials and preparation
- Audio library – songs
- Puppet
- Visual schedule pictures

Stand together in a circle and sing the *Hello song* (track 2). Say *hello* to the puppet and ask, *How are you?*
Remind students of the attention-getter, *1, 2, 3 It's time for... CBeebies!* Remind students that they should be quiet and pay attention whenever you say this.
Show the visual schedule pictures and invite the class helper to help you pick out the ones that represent what you will do today.

> **Note to teachers**
> Introduce high fives, handshakes, and hugs and allow students to select which greeting they want to receive.

### Make a word list.

Stand together in a circle. Tell students you are going to say a word. Say, for example, *kitchen*. The student says on your left your word and adds another word. Then the next student says both words and adds another. Continue around the circle. Allow students to use any words they know in English.

CBeebies

# ACTIVE LEARNING

### Before watching the video – Messy places

#### Materials and preparation
- Printouts of a messy bedroom (toys everywhere), a kitchen with lots of dirty dishes, and another messy bedroom (clothes everywhere)

Sit together in a circle and show students each printout. Ask students what they can see and what needs to be done. Stick the pictures up on the wall and divide the class into three groups. Each group stands at one card and mime the actions of tidying up, doing the dishes, and putting clothes away. Rotate the groups around so every group has a turn at each picture.

> **Note to teachers**
> Encourage students to say, *What are we going to do?*, *We need to tidy up*, and *Ready to tidy up?*

### Watching the video - Let's watch!

#### Materials and preparation
- Video library

Sit together in a semicircle and make sure every student can see the screen. Play *Sarah and Duck Series 2, Ep 13, Toy Tidy* (Video 9). Watch the video together. Watch the video again and stop to ask students what toys they can see and where the toys are. Ask students where the toys belong and together mime tidying up.

You should set expectations of correct watching behavior, reminding students that they should sit still and watch quietly, respecting their classmates.

### After watching the video – Make a mini-book.

#### Materials and preparation
- Colored pencils or crayons
- Construction paper (one sheet per student)
- Pencils

Sit students at their tables and give each student a sheet of construction paper. Help them fold the paper in two to make a mini-book. On the first page, invite students to draw toys in Duck's drawers, on the second page, students draw a sink with dishes, and on the third page, they draw clothes in a wardrobe.

> **Note to teachers**
> To support students, show them pictures, draw each page item first together, or play the video again and pause at different points.

# DIFFERENTIATED INSTRUCTION

### BELOW LEVEL
**After watching the video**
If students struggle with folding the mini-book, give them four halves of A4 paper.

### ABOVE LEVEL
**After watching the video**
Once students have finished, put them into pairs and invite them to show, share, and describe their mini-book pages.

# CLOSING

### Talk about the videos. Sing the *Goodbye song*.

#### Materials and preparation
- Audio library – songs

Talk with students about the three videos they watched in the unit. Encourage them to recall/act out what they saw in each video and say which was their favorite. Sing the *Goodbye song* (track 3) and invite students to sing along. Say *goodbye* to them and have them say *goodbye* back to you.

# Unit 4 Why do we feel hot or cold?

### Learning goals
- Make connections between the weather and the clothes we wear
- Categorize clothes according to hot and cold weather
- Understand familiar words in a video

### Main language content
Clothes: *coat, gloves, sandals, sunglasses, sweater, T-shirt, woolly hat*
*Do you wear (sandals) when it's (hot/cold)?*
*It's (hot/cold).*

## OPENING

### Circle time

**Materials and preparation**
- Audio library – songs
- Puppet
- Visual schedule pictures

Stand together in a circle and sing the *Hello song* (track 2). Say *hello* to the puppet and ask, *How are you?*
Remind students of the attention-getter, *Everybody look at me, it's time for CBeebies!* Remind students that they should be quiet and pay attention whenever you say this.
Show the visual schedule pictures and invite the class helper to help you pick out the ones that represent what you will do today.

> **Note to teachers**
> Introduce high fives, handshakes, and hugs and allow students to select which greeting they want to receive.

### My clothes

**Materials and preparation**
- Fly swatters (x2)
- Printouts or real clothes: sandals, woolly hat, gloves, sunglasses, T-shirt, sweater, coat

Show students the printouts or clothes. Elicit or say the word for each one and encourage students to join in. Mix up the pictures/clothes and lay them face up in the middle of the circle. Give two students the fly swatters and call out an item of clothing. Students find it and touch the card lightly with the fly swatter. Move students around so every student has turn. Make sure to set expectations of using the fly swatters correctly and do not leave students unsupervised with them.

32 CBeebies

# ACTIVE LEARNING

### Before watching the video – What do we wear in hot and cold weather?
### Materials and preparation
- Clothes for hot and cold weather (optional)
- Flashcards: *cold, hot*
- Printouts: sandals, woolly hat, gloves, sunglasses, T-shirt, sweater, coat

Sit together in a circle. Show students the *hot* and *cold* flashcards. Mime feeling hot (sweating) and feeling cold (shivering). Say the words and encourage students to join in saying the words and acting out. Lay the other printouts in the middle of the circle and ask students what they wear when it is hot and cold. Stick all the pictures on the walls randomly and stand together in the middle. Call out, *It's hot!* and students run to any clothes item they can wear in hot weather. Repeat with *cold*.
You should set expectations of moving safely so as to avoid accidents.

> **Note to teachers**
> Bring in real clothing if you can and allow students to try on the clothes and say, *It's (hot/cold)*.

### Watching the video - Let's watch!
### Materials and preparation
- Video library

Sit together in a semicircle so everyone can see the screen. Play *Kit & Pup, Series 1, Hot & Cold* (Video 10). Watch the video together. Watch the video again and stop after each piece of clothing is shown to answer *hot* or *cold* and say the name of the different items.
You should set expectations of correct watching behavior, reminding students that they should sit still and watch quietly, respecting their classmates.

### After watching the video – Match the clothes
### Materials and preparation
- Colored pens
- Pencils
- Project Book page 17

Sit students at their tables. Help students open their Project Books to page 17. Go over each item of clothing together and say, *It's for (hot/cold) weather*. Show students how to draw a line from the clothes to the hot or the cold symbol on the page. Give students a pencil each. Have students look, think, and match the clothes to the corresponding weather.

> **Note to teachers**
> Fast finishers can color the clothes.

# DIFFERENTIATED INSTRUCTION

### BELOW LEVEL
### Before watching the video
Focus only on the clothes from the video, working with only four vocabulary items and matching those to hot or cold weather. Simplify the input language by using only *hot* and *cold*.

### ABOVE LEVEL
### After watching the video
Invite students to think of and draw more clothes on the hot and cold parts of the page.

# CLOSING

### Is it hot or cold? Sing the *Goodbye song*.
### Materials and preparation
- Audio library – songs

Mime being hot and ask students, *Hot or cold?* Encourage them to answer and mime being hot. Repeat with cold. Sing the *Goodbye song* (track 3) and invite students to sing along while they put their things away. Encourage students to help each other and take responsibility for the classroom environment. Say *goodbye* to them and have them say *goodbye* back to you.

### Learning goals
- Make connections between the weather and the clothes we wear
- Express preference in relation to clothes
- Use visuals to understand a video

### Main language content
Clothes: *sandals, woolly hat, gloves, sunglasses, T-shirt, sweater, coat*
Colors
*It's (hot/cold).*
*This is my favorite.*

## OPENING

### Circle time

### Materials and preparation
- Audio library – songs
- Puppet
- Weather chart

Stand together in a circle and sing the *Hello song* (track 2). Say *hello* to the puppet and ask, *How are you?* Everyone asks each other. Use the Weather chart to ask, *What's the weather like?* Students point to the weather and act it out.

> **Note to teachers**
> Focus on the clothes students are wearing and together connect it to the weather.

Remind students of the attention-getter, *Everybody look at me, it's time for CBeebies!* Remind students that they should be quiet and pay attention whenever you say this.

Show the visual schedule pictures and invite the class helper to help you pick out the ones that represent what you will do today.

### Listen and draw.

### Materials and preparation
- Colored pencils
- Printouts: *sandals, woolly hat, gloves, sunglasses, T-shirt, sweater, coat*
- Sheets of paper (one per student)

Stick the clothes printouts on the board. Give students a sheet of A4 paper and put the colored pencils in the middle of the table. Students put the page landscape in front of them and draw a line straight down the middle. Tell students on the left there's a girl and it's hot so she's wearing a T-shirt, sandals, and sunglasses. On the right there's a boy and it's cold so he's wearing a woolly hat, sweater, and gloves. Students listen and draw.

## ACTIVE LEARNING

### Before watching the video – Look and say.

**Materials and preparation**
- Printouts: sandals, woolly hat, gloves, sunglasses, T-shirt, sweater, coat

Sit together in a circle and slowly reveal each of the printouts. Encourage students to say what they can see. Lay the pictures in a line in the middle of the circle and say the words together. Tell students to close their eyes. Take away a printout at random. Students open their eyes and tell you which picture is missing. Continue until all the printouts are gone.

> **Note to teachers**
> Ask students about their favorite clothes and tell them about your favorite clothes.

### Watching the video - Let's watch!

**Materials and preparation**
- Video library

Sit together in a semicircle so everyone can see the screen. Play *Kit & Pup, Series 1, Hot & Cold* (Video 10). Watch the video together. Watch it again and stop to categorize hot and cold weather clothes together. Stop and say the clothes you see. You should set expectations of correct watching behavior, reminding students that they should sit still and watch quietly, respecting their classmates.

### After watching the video – Design a sweater.

**Materials and preparation**
- Colored markers
- Different craft materials (felt, ribbon, crepe paper, etc.)
- Glue
- Scissors
- Sweater template (draw an outline of the front and back of a sweater on a sheet of A4 paper and make copies, one per student)

Sit students at their tables and give each student a sweater template. Put the glue, scissors, colored pens, and different materials in the middle of the table. Tell students they can design their favorite sweater using whatever materials and colors they want.

> **Note to teachers**
> Encourage students to mix and match colors and materials for creative and imaginative development.

## DIFFERENTIATED INSTRUCTION

### BELOW LEVEL
### Before watching the video

You can cut the paper into two halves before the class and give each student two halves if you think they will struggle with identifying and drawing on the right and left sides of one sheet of paper.

### ABOVE LEVEL
### After watching the video

Sit together in a circle with the finished sweater design craft. Students show and share their sweater designs, describing colors and patterns.

## CLOSING

### Say what you are wearing. Sing the *Goodbye song*.

**Materials and preparation**
- Audio library – songs

Encourage students to describe what they are wearing. Ask students if it's hot or cold and relate it to the clothes everyone is wearing. Sing the *Goodbye song* (track 3) and invite students to sing along while they put their things away. Say *goodbye* to them and have them say *goodbye* back to you.

### Learning goals
- Practice saying words for clothes
- Identify purpose and size differences in context
- Use visuals to understand a video

### Main language content
Clothes: *coat, raincoat*
Colors
Sizes: *too (big/small)*
*It's a* (blue) (*coat/umbrella/raincoat*).

## OPENING

### Circle time

#### Materials and preparation
- Puppet
- Days of the Week poster
- Weather flashcards

Stand together in a circle and sing the *Hello song* (track 2). Say *hello* to the puppet and ask, *How are you?* Everyone asks each other.
Remind students of the attention-getter, *Everybody look at me, it's time for CBeebies!* Remind students that they should be quiet and pay attention whenever you say this.
Show the visual schedule pictures and invite the class helper to help you pick out the ones that represent what you will do today.

> **Note to teachers**
> Remind students of the other attention-getters that they know.

### Getting dressed for rainy weather

#### Materials and preparation
- Printouts: rain, raincoat, umbrella
- Video of the song *Rain, rain, go away* (optional, found on the Internet)

Sit together in a circle and slowly reveal the printouts. Say the words and encourage students to join in. Spread the pictures in the middle of the circle. Hold up the rain printout and mime the rain; encourage students to join in. Repeat with the umbrella printout and mime opening an umbrella. Then repeat with the raincoat and mime putting on a raincoat. Do this several times, alternating between the pictures. Encourage students to join in saying the words and miming the actions.

> **Note to teachers**
> You may like to find a video of the song *Rain, rain, go away* on the Internet, play it for students, and encourage them to sing and join in with miming telling the rain to go away.

# ACTIVE LEARNING

## Before watching the video – Trying on coats

### Materials and preparation
- Coats (different sizes, materials, colors, and for different weather conditions; alternatively you can use pictures)

Sit together in a circle and look at the different coats together. Ask students to feel and try on the coats. Focus on size (*too big* and *too small*) and the colors. Ask students what coat to wear when it's hot, cold, and raining and decide together.

> **Note to teachers**
> Use different pictures if you can't use real coats. If it is a rainy/cold day on the day of the class and students are wearing coats/sweaters, you can incorporate these.

## Watching the video - Let's watch!

### Materials and preparation
- Video library

Sit together in a semicircle so everyone can see the screen. Play *Yakka Dee, Series 3, Ep 6, Coat* (Video 11). Watch the video together. Watch it again and stop to talk about the size and color of the coats in the video. Stop and ask students what weather each coat is for.
You should set expectations of correct watching behavior, reminding students that they should sit still and watch quietly, respecting their classmates.

## After watching the video – Look, think, and draw.

### Materials and preparation
- Colored markers
- Pencil
- Project Book page 19

Sit students at their tables. Help them open their Project Books to page 19. Point to the coats and elicit the color and the size of each one in the sequence. Ask, *What coat is next?* and encourage students to answer. Give students a pencil each and put the colored markers in the middle of the table. Ask students to look, think, and draw to complete the sequences.

> **Note to teachers**
> Encourage students to say the color of coats they see in the sequence to give further practice and cement language.

# DIFFERENTIATED INSTRUCTION

## BELOW LEVEL
### Before watching the video

### Materials and preparation
- Printouts of different colored coats that are the same size and type

Look at color only and don't focus on size and weather. Use printouts of different colored coats that are the same size and type. Encourage students to say, *It's a (blue) coat*.

## ABOVE LEVEL
### After watching the video

### Materials and preparation
- Sheets of paper

Ask students to invent a sequence of their own on a separate sheet of paper and switch it with another student for them to complete the sequence.

# CLOSING

## Sing *Rain, rain, go away*. Say goodbye.

### Materials and preparation
- Video of the song *Rain, rain, go away* (found on the Internet)

Play a video/the audio of the song *Rain, rain, go away* (this can easily be found on the Internet). Encourage students to join in and sing. Then play the song again and change *Rain, rain, go away* to *Let's go home and play*. Say *goodbye* to the students and have them say *goodbye* back to you.

## OPENING

### Circle time

### Materials and preparation
- Audio library – songs
- Puppet
- Visual schedule pictures

Stand together in a circle and sing the *Hello song* (track 2). Say *hello* to the puppet and ask, *How are you?* Everyone asks each other. Remind students of the attention-getter, *Everybody look at me, it's time for CBeebies!* Remind students that they should be quiet and pay attention whenever you say this.
Show the visual schedule pictures and invite the class helper to help you pick out the ones that represent what you will do today.

> **Note to teachers**
> Remind students of the other attention-getters that they know.

### Sing *What's the weather like today?*

### Materials and preparation
- Audio library – songs

Stand together in a circle. Play the *What's the weather like today?* song (track 13). Encourage students to sing, dance, and do the actions. Ask students, *Where does rain come from?* and encourage them to say *clouds*.

### Learning goals
- Understand, observe and record the weather outside
- Identify different clouds and their function
- Give their opinion on a video

### Main language content
Adjective: *fluffy*
Weather: *cloud, rain, rain cloud, rain drops, shades*
*It's raining.*
*It's cloudy/sunny/rainy.*
*Need to stay cool.*

## ACTIVE LEARNING

### Before watching the video – Talking about clouds

#### Materials and preparation
- Board markers (black and blue)

Draw a cloud on the board. Say *cloud* and have students repeat. Then color the cloud in black and say, *Oh, no! It's a rain cloud.* Invite students to say what will happen. Draw raindrops and say, *It's raining.* Ask, *How do you feel when it's raining?* Encourage them to share their ideas. Then erase the raindrops and the black cloud, and draw a sun coming out. Say, *It's sunny* and ask students to share how they feel when it's sunny.

> **Note to teachers**
> Encourage students to talk about what they know about rain and where rain comes from.

### Watching the video - Let's watch!

#### Materials and preparation
- Video library

Sit together in a semicircle and make sure every student can see the screen. Play *Sarah and Duck Series 2, Ep 3, Cloud Tower* (Video 12). Watch the video together. Watch the video again and stop when you see shade and rain clouds. Ask students where the clouds are in the video. You should set expectations of correct watching behavior, reminding students that they should sit still and watch quietly, respecting their classmates.

### After watching the video – Make a rain cloud.

#### Materials and preparation
- Construction paper
- Glue
- Gray crepe paper
- Light blue wool
- Popsicle sticks
- Scissors

Sit students at their tables. Give students a sheet of construction paper and ask them to draw a big cloud. Help them to cut out the cloud. Tell students it's a big rain cloud and invite them to stick the gray crepe paper on the cloud. Use the blue wool to stick on the bottom of the cloud as rain. Help them stick the cloud on a popsicle stick.

> **Note to teachers**
> Encourage students to sing *Rain, rain, go away* (from the previous class) as they are making the cloud.

## DIFFERENTIATED INSTRUCTION

### BELOW LEVEL
**After watching the video**
Draw and cut out the cloud for students if they struggle to do this independently.

### ABOVE LEVEL
**Before watching the video**
Show students the water cycle by drawing it on the board.

## CLOSING

### Talk about the videos. Sing the *Goodbye song*.

#### Materials and preparation
- Audio library – songs

Talk with students about the three videos they watched in the unit. Encourage them to recall/act out what they saw in each video and say which was their favorite. Sing the *Goodbye song* (track 3) and invite students to sing along. Say *goodbye* to them and have them say *goodbye* back to you.

# Unit 5 What other living things are around us?

## OPENING

### Circle time

**Materials and preparation**
- Audio library – songs
- Puppet
- Visual schedule pictures

Stand together in a circle and sing the *Hello song* (track 2). Say *hello* to the puppet and ask, *How are you?*
Remind students of the attention-getter, *Everybody look at me, it's time for CBeebies!* Remind students that they should be quiet and pay attention whenever you say this.
Show the visual schedule pictures and invite the class helper to help you pick out the ones that represent what you will do today.

> **Note to teachers**
> Introduce high fives, handshakes, and hugs and allow students to select which greeting they want to receive.

### Sing *Itsy Bitsy Spider.*

**Materials and preparation**
- Video of the song *Itsy Bitsy Spider* (found on the Internet)

Play students a video or the audio of the song *Itsy Bitsy Spider* and sing together. Mime using your hands to represent the spider. Repeat and act out being the spider and the sun coming out. Encourage students to join in.

**Learning goals**
- Learn to recognize and name some of the creatures that live in the garden
- Develop creative and motor skills in context
- Use visuals to understand a video

**Main language content**
Adjectives: *slow, speedy*
Animals: *ladybug, snail, spider, worm*
Colors
Size: *long, little*
In the garden,

## ACTIVE LEARNING

### Before watching the video – Listen and run.

**Materials and preparation**
- A magnifying glass (optional)
- Printouts: garden, worm, spider, ladybird, snail

Sit together in a circle and slowly reveal each printout. Stick the pictures of the bugs up around the room and stand together in the middle. Call out an animal and students run to the correct picture. Put the garden picture at the front of the class, hold up (or mime holding) a magnifying glass, and tell students you're going to look for animals. Go around class together, find the bugs, and say their names. Encourage students to repeat the words and mime the bugs' actions.
You should set expectations of moving safely so as to avoid accidents.

> **Note to teachers**
> Extend by asking students if the animals are little or long, slow or fast. Mime being the bugs together.

### Watching the video

**Materials and preparation**
- Video library

Sit together in a semicircle so everyone can see the screen. *Play Yakka Dee, Series 1, Ep 11 Worm* (Video 13). Watch the video together. Watch it and stop each time there's a worm. Mime being the worm and the type (long or little, slow or speedy). You should set expectations of correct watching behavior, reminding students that they should sit still and watch quietly, respecting their classmates.

> **Note to teachers**
> Students may have already heard the word *fast*. Make sure they understand that *speedy* is another word for *fast*.

### After watching the video – Make a worm.

**Materials and preparation**
- Colored construction paper (cut into circles to make a worm)
- Colored markers
- Glue
- Popsicle sticks (one per student)
- Scissors

Sit students at their tables and put the construction paper, glue, and scissors in the middle of the table. Give them the colored circles. Help them stick them together to make a worm. Stick a popsicle stick at the front and back of the worm. When they finish, students play with their worms together. They can race each other, making their worms speedy or slow.

## DIFFERENTIATED INSTRUCTION

### BELOW LEVEL
**After watching the video**
Show students how to draw a whole worm, rather than stick together pieces to create the worm. Focus on the worm being long. Together act out *slow* and *speedy*.

### ABOVE LEVEL
**After watching the video**
Invite students to act out a bug from the video in front of the class for the other students to guess.

## CLOSING

### Sing *Itsy Bitsy Spider*.

**Materials and preparation**
- Video of the song *Itsy Bitsy Spider* (found on the Internet)

Play the *Itsy Bitsy Spider* video again and invite students to sing along while they clean up. Encourage students to help each other, put away the craft things in the correct place, and take responsibility for the classroom environment. Say *goodbye* to them and have them say *goodbye* back to you.

**Learning goals**
- Learn to recognize and name some of the creatures that live in the garden
- Develop creative and imaginative skills in context
- Give their opinion on a video

**Main language content**
Adjectives: *slow, speedy*
Animals: *ladybug, snail, spider, worm*
*little, long*
*I (don't) like (worms).*
*In the garden.*

# OPENING

## Circle time

**Materials and preparation**
- Puppet
- Days of the Week poster
- Weather flashcards

Stand together in a circle and sing the *Hello song* (track 2). Say *hello* to the puppet and ask, *How are you?* Everyone asks each other.
Remind students of the attention-getter, *Everybody look at me, it's time for CBeebies!*
Remind students that they should be quiet and pay attention whenever you say this.
Show the visual schedule pictures and invite the class helper to help you pick out the ones that represent what you will do today.

> **Note to teachers**
> Remind students of the other attention-getters that they know.

## Slow or speedy?

Remind students of the words *slow* and *speedy* from the previous class. Ask them to pretend to be spiders and move around the classroom. Call out *slow* and *speedy*, and have students change their speed accordingly. You should set expectations of moving safely so as to avoid accidents.

> **Note to teachers**
> Ask students to move like other bugs, such as worms.

CBeebies

# ACTIVE LEARNING

### Before watching the video – Listen and run.

### Materials and preparation
- Fly swatters (x2)
- Printouts: garden, worm, spider, ladybug, snail

Sit together in a circle. Slowly reveal each of the printouts. Stick them on the board, organize students into two groups, line them up facing the board. Give the first two students in each line one of the fly swatters. Call out one of the cards, students race and swat the correct card. Continue with the next two students in the line. You should set expectations of moving safely so as to avoid accidents.

> **Note to teachers**
> With larger classes make three groups so students don't have to wait too long to have a turn. If you don't have fly swatters, students can simply touch the pictures.

### Watching the video – Let's watch!

### Materials and preparation
- Video library

Sit together in a semicircle so everyone can see the screen. Play *Yakka Dee, Series 1, Ep 11 Worm* (Video 13). Watch the video together. Watch it and stop at each worm to ask students what color and size it is. Ask students if it's slow or speedy and compare with the other animals. You should set expectations of correct watching behavior, reminding students that they should sit still and watch quietly, respecting their classmates.

### After watching the video – Snail painting

### Materials and preparation
- A4 cardstock paper (half a sheet per student)
- Colored water paints
- Pencils
- Paintbrushes
- Popsicle sticks (one per student; optional)

Sit students at their tables and put the watercolors in the middle of the table. Give each student half a sheet of A4 card and a pencil each. Together draw a big snail. Invite students to use the paints to color the snail shell.

> **Note to teachers**
> Students can cut out the snail and stick it on a popsicle stick to carry it around and act out being snails.

# DIFFERENTIATED INSTRUCTION

### BELOW LEVEL
### Before watching the video
Play a few rounds of a memory game before the activity: Place the pictures face down, turning them over at random for students to see the picture and repeat the word. This gives students more chance to recognize the words.

### ABOVE LEVEL
### Before watching the video
Extend the activity by playing *Say it and pass it on*. Give a picture to a student on your left and another picture to a student on your right. Continue passing the pictures in both directions while students say the word.

# CLOSING

### Toy racing. Sing the *Goodbye song*.

### Materials and preparation
- A selection of wind-up toys (at least two)
- A short rope or masking tape
- Audio library – songs

Sit with students in a circle. Place two wind-up toys in the middle. Some distance away, place some rope or mark a line with masking tape. Tell students that the toys are going to have a race. Ask them to guess which toy is *speedy* and which one is *slow*. Invite two students to wind up the toys and put them on the line to start moving. Check if students' predictions were correct at the end of the race. Repeat this until you have used all of the toys. Play the *Goodbye song* (track 3) and encourage students to sing along. Say *goodbye* to them and have them say *goodbye* back to you.

Unit 5

**Learning goals**
- Describe the appearance and behavior of insects
- Understand the stages of development of a butterfly
- Use visuals to understand a video

**Main language content**
Colors
Nature: *butterfly, caterpillar, cocoon, leaf; fly, munch, sleep, wiggle*

# OPENING

### Circle time

**Materials and preparation**
- Audio library – songs
- Puppet
- Visual schedule pictures

Stand together in a circle and sing the *Hello song* (track 2). Say *hello* to the puppet and ask, *How are you?* Everyone asks each other.
Remind students of the attention-getter, *Everybody look at me, it's time for CBeebies!* Remind students that they should be quiet and pay attention whenever you say this.
Show the visual schedule pictures and invite the class helper to help you pick out the ones that represent what you will do today.

> **Note to teachers**
> Remind students of the other attention-getters that they know.

### Caterpillars and butterflies

**Materials and preparation**
- Printouts of caterpillars and butterflies

Sit in a circle with students. Show the printouts and say *caterpillar* and *butterfly*. Explore the pictures with students. Ask them what colors and sizes they can see. Encourage their interest in the development process. Ask, *How do you think a caterpillar becomes a butterfly?*

# ACTIVE LEARNING

### Before watching the video – How does a caterpillar become a butterfly?

### Materials and preparation

- Printouts: caterpillar, leaf, cocoon, butterfly

Stick the printouts in order of the butterfly development (*caterpillar, leaf, cocoon, butterfly*) along the wall at the front of the classroom. Tell students that you are going to explain how a caterpillar becomes a butterfly. Ask them, *Do you want to come on this journey with me?* Invite them to stand up and move to the *caterpillar* picture with you. Say *caterpillar* and mime wiggling. Say *wiggle, wiggle* as you do the action. Move together to the picture of the *leaf* and say the word. Mime *munching* while saying *munch, munch*. Move to the picture of the cocoon and say the word. Mime sleeping while saying *sleep, sleep*. Move to the picture of the butterfly, say the word, and mime being a butterfly. Encourage students to join in with all of the movements.

> **Note to teachers**
> Ask students about what bugs they like and what bugs they've seen in nature. Ask them how they react when they see a bug. Do they get scared?

### Watching the video – Let's watch!
### Materials and preparation

- Video library

Sit together in a semicircle so everyone can see the screen. Play *Show Me Show Me, Series 1, Ep 20, Caterpillars and Cake* (Video 14). Watch the video together. Watch it again and stop at each of the stages of the caterpillar; ask what students can see and together say it and mime the actions.
You should set expectations of correct watching behavior, reminding students that they should sit still and watch quietly, respecting their classmates.

### After watching the video – Look, think, draw, and color.
### Materials and preparation

- Colored markers
- Crepe paper
- Glue
- Pencils
- Scissors
- Project Book page 21

Sit students at their tables. Help students open their Project Books to page 21 and look at the pictures. Go over each item together. Put the colored pens and crepe paper in the middle of the table. Tell students to draw a leaf next to the caterpillar. Next, students trace round the caterpillar and the cocoon and color them. Finally, students use the crepe paper to cut pieces and make wings for the butterfly to stick them on.

> **Note to teachers**
> Fast finishers can work in groups or pairs and act out the stages together, using the Project Book page as a prompt.

# DIFFERENTIATED INSTRUCTION

### BELOW LEVEL
### Before watching the video

Focus only on *caterpillar, cocoon,* and *butterfly* and mime without adding further vocabulary, like *wiggle, munch, sleep,* and *fly*.

### ABOVE LEVEL
### After watching the video

Invite students number the pictures in order.

# CLOSING

### Show and tell. Sing the *Goodbye song.*

### Materials and preparation

- Audio library – songs
- Project Book page 21

Sit in a circle with students and invite them to show their books to each other and describe their butterflies. Encourage them to use words for colors and sizes. Sing the *Goodbye song* (track 3) and encourage students to join in and sing. Say *goodbye* to them and have them say *goodbye* back to you.

# OPENING

## Circle time

### Materials and preparation
- Audio library – songs
- Puppet
- Visual schedule pictures

Stand together in a circle and sing the *Hello song* (track 2). Say *hello* to the puppet and ask, *How are you?*
Remind students of the attention-getter, *Everybody look at me, it's time for CBeebies!* Remind students that they should be quiet and pay attention whenever you say this.
Show the visual schedule pictures and invite the class helper to help you pick out the ones that represent what you will do today.

> **Note to teachers**
> Introduce high fives, handshakes, and hugs and allow students to select which greeting they want to receive.

### Play *Guess the animal.*

Sit together in a circle. Mime an animal that students are familiar with for students to guess. Invite students to mime an animal for the class to guess.

### Learning goals
- Understand that plants are living things with specific needs and describe its life cycle
- Identify the stages of plant growth in context
- Give their opinion on a video

### Main language content
Nature: *seeds, shallots; dig a hole, cover the hole, plant seeds, wait*
*Let's see what grows.*

CBeebies

# ACTIVE LEARNING

### Before watching the video – Let's plant!

### Materials and preparation
- A package of seeds
- A tray with soil in it
- A water can

If possible, take students to the garden. Sit together in a circle. Show the package of seeds and mime opening it. Make a small hole in the soil, drop the seed in, and cover it up. Ask, *What does the seed need to grow?* Encourage students to say, *water* and *sun.* Mime watering the seed with the watering can. Ask students to imagine what will grow from the soil and describe it. Students can talk about flowers, fruits, or vegetables — all of these are valid options. Encourage all students to participate.

> **Note to teachers**
> Talk with students about whether they have ever planted something at home or at a family member's house. Is there a garden where they live? What do people plant there?

### Watching the video - Let's watch!

### Materials and preparation
- Video library

Sit together in a semicircle and make sure every student can see the screen.

Play *Sarah and Duck Series 1 Ep 1 Lots of Shallots* (Video 15). Watch the video together. Watch the video again and stop to mime the planting actions together. You should set expectations of correct watching behavior, reminding students that they should sit still and watch quietly, respecting their classmates.

### After watching the video – Look, find, and stick.

### Materials and preparation
- Colored markers
- Pencils
- Project Book page 23

Sit students at their tables. Help students open their Project Books to page 23 and say what they can see. Show students the shallots on the sticker page and invite students to match and stick on the shallots. Help students with the stickers as needed.

> **Note to teachers**
> Fast finishers can draw any other vegetables or plants they can think of on the vegetable patch.

# DIFFERENTIATED INSTRUCTION

### BELOW LEVEL
### Guess the animal.

Use printouts/pictures to prompt students and help them if they struggle to think of an animal. Reinforce the language as needed.

### ABOVE LEVEL
### After watching the video

Ask students to draw a sun and watering can on the picture. Encourage students to remember the other root vegetables in the video story and draw them on the picture.

# CLOSING

### Talk about the videos. Sing the *Goodbye song.*

### Materials and preparation
- Audio library – songs

Talk with students about the three videos they watched in the unit. Encourage them to recall/act out what they saw in each video and say which was their favorite. Sing the *Goodbye song* (track 3) and invite students to sing along. Say *goodbye* to them and have them say *goodbye* back to you.

# Unit 6 Why is food important?

### Learning goals
- Talk about food items and healthy food
- Identify and recognize vegetables that grow underground and above ground
- Give their opinion on a video

### Main language content
Vegetables: *broccoli, carrots, onions, turnips; above ground, underground*
*I (don't) like (carrots).*
*Yummy, yummy in my tummy!*

## OPENING

### Circle time

**Materials and preparation**
- Audio library – songs
- Puppet
- Visual schedule

Stand together in a circle and sing the *Hello song* (track 2). Say *hello* to the puppet and ask, *How are you?* Pass the puppet around to students and they ask each other and answer.
Ask students what they did yesterday evening and what food they had for dinner. Use the puppet as a model, for example:
**Puppet:** *I had chicken for dinner yesterday.*
**Teacher:** *Yummy! I like chicken. My dinner was pasta.*

> **Note to teachers**
> Encourage students to listen to each other and talk about what food they like and why.

Show the visual schedule pictures and invite the class helper to help you pick out the ones that represent what you will do today.

### Let's find the vegetables!

**Materials and preparation**
- Printouts: carrots, turnips, onions, broccoli

Slowly reveal each of the vegetable printouts. Tell students to close their eyes while you go around the classroom hiding the vegetable printouts. Ask students to open their eyes and find them. You should set expectations of walking safely so as to avoid accidents.

> **Note to teachers**
> If you have a very large class, you can organize students into small groups and invite different groups to find the pictures, hiding them in different places each time.

## ACTIVE LEARNING

### Before watching the video – Yummy, yummy!

**Materials and preparation**
- Printouts: carrots, turnips, onions, broccoli

Sit together in a circle and slow reveal each of the vegetable printouts. Put the printouts in a line in front of the class, pick up the picture and say, *I like broccoli.* and *Yummy, yummy!* Invite students to do the same. Repeat with other pictures and also with *I don't like*. Stick the pictures around the room, call out, *I like…* and students run to any vegetable they like and say its name. Repeat it with *I don't like*.

> **Note to teachers**
> Extend by adding a description of the vegetable, by saying its color and size.

### Watching the video – Let's watch!

**Materials and preparation**
- Video library

Sit together in a semicircle so everyone can see the screen. Play *Kit & Pup, Series 1, Ep 49 Vegetables* (Video 16). Watch the video together. Watch it and stop each time you see a vegetable. Ask students if they like it or don't like it. Focus on *underground* and *above ground* and mime together.
You should set expectations of correct watching behavior, reminding students that they should sit still and watch quietly, respecting their classmates.

### After watching the video – Make a vegetable garden.

**Materials and preparation**
- Colored pencils
- Crayons
- Crêpe paper (green and blue; optional)
- Paper plates (one per student)
- Pictures: broccoli, carrots, onions, turnips

Sit students at their tables. Put the crepe paper and colored pencils in the middle of the table. Give students a paper plate each and draw a line down the middle of the plate. Ask students what vegetables grow underground and use the pictures to help. Students draw carrots, turnips, and onions below the line. Ask students what vegetable grows above ground; students should draw broccoli.

> **Note to teachers**
> Fast finishers can color the sky and ground and add green for the carrots, turnips, and onions using crepe paper.

## DIFFERENTIATED INSTRUCTION

### BELOW LEVEL
**After watching the video**

Focus on the vegetables only; do not focus too much on *above* and *under*.

### ABOVE LEVEL
**After watching the video**

Students can draw other vegetables on their plates.

## CLOSING

### Talk about vegetables. Sing the *Goodbye song*.

**Materials and preparation**
- A bag or pillowcase
- Audio library – songs
- Different root vegetables (real or plastic)

Put the root vegetables in a bag/pillowcase. Sit students in a circle and have them pass the bag/pillowcase around, feel a root vegetable, guess, and then take it out. Talk about the root vegetables, asking students to name them and say whether they saw them in the video.
Sing the *Goodbye song* (track 3) and encourage students to sing along. Say *goodbye* to them and have them say *goodbye* back to you.

### Learning goals
- Talk about food items and healthy food
- Understand simple plant growth through experiments
- Understand an animated video

### Main language content
Plant growth: *sun, water; above ground*
Vegetables: *broccoli, carrots, watercress, onions, turnips*

## OPENING

### Circle time

**Materials and preparation**
- Audio library – songs
- Puppet
- Visual schedule pictures

Stand together in a circle and sing the *Hello song* (track 2). Say *hello* to the puppet and ask, *How are you?*
Remind students of the attention-getter, *Everybody look at me, it's time for CBeebies!* Remind students that they should be quiet and pay attention whenever you say this.
Show the visual schedule pictures and invite the class helper to help you pick out the ones that represent what you will do today.

> **Note to teachers**
> Introduce high fives, handshakes, and hugs and allow students to select which greeting they want to receive.

### Let's draw vegetables!

**Materials and preparation**
- A4 sheets of construction paper with four equal boxes draw on them (one per student)
- Colored pencils
- Scissors

Sit students at their tables and give students a sheet of construction paper. Have students observe the four equal boxes. Tell students there are three carrots in box 1. Students select the right color and draw the carrots. Continue with two turnips in box 2, five onions in box 3, and one head of broccoli in box 4. Then students cut up the construction paper to make mini-cards.

> **Note to teachers**
> If students aren't confident about cutting, you can skip this step.

## ACTIVE LEARNING

### Before watching the video – Growing plants

**Materials and preparation**
- Printouts: garden, seeds, watering can, water, sun, plants growing

Sit together in a circle and show students the different printouts in sequence of how to grow plants. Together act out planting seeds, watering them, being sunshine, and watching them grow. Mix the printouts up and invite students to reorganize them in sequence.

> **Note to teachers**
> If possible, take students out into the playground/yard to look for grass, weeds, and plants to find and look at roots together.

### Watching the video - Let's watch!

**Materials and preparation**
- Video library

Sit together in a semicircle so everyone can see the screen. Play *Kit & Pup, Series 1, Ep 49 Vegetables* (Video 16). Watch the video together. Watch it again and stop at the vegetables and say the name and if they grow above ground or under ground. Stop and ask what plants need to grow and focus on water and light.
You should set expectations of correct watching behavior, reminding students that they should sit still and watch quietly, respecting their classmates.

### After watching the video – Let's grow watercress.

**Materials and preparation**
- Cress seeds
- Paper cups (one per student)
- Paper towel
- Permanent markers

Give students a paper cup each and tell students you're going to grow watercress. Together wet the paper towel and stuff it in the paper cups. Students sprinkle lots of watercress seeds on the paper towel in the cups. Give students a permanent marker each to write their name on the cups and draw a face. Put the cups on a windowsill in class.

> **Note to teachers**
> If you do not have access to watercress, any other fast growing vegetable could be used.

## DIFFERENTIATED INSTRUCTION

### BELOW LEVEL
**Let's draw vegetables!**
Precut the construction paper for students and keep the vegetables to one, instead of stating different numbers. Provide support by telling students the color of the vegetables.

### ABOVE LEVEL
**Let's draw vegetables!**
Once students have their set of mini-cards, put them in pairs or small groups and have them play the memory game together. Students lay all their cards face down and match the vegetables.

## CLOSING

### Look and say. Sing the *Goodbye song.*

**Materials and preparation**
- Audio library – songs

Start drawing a vegetable on the board and encourage students to say its name before you finish drawing. Repeat with other vegetables and food items.
Sing the *Goodbye song* (track 3) and invite students to sing along while they put their things away. Encourage students to help each other and take responsibility for the classroom environment. Say *goodbye* to them and have them say *goodbye* back to you.

**Learning goals**
- Talk about utensils we use to eat
- Express preferences in context
- Understand familiar words in a video

**Main language content**
Utensils: *fork, knife, spoon (dessert spoon, soup spoon, teaspoon, wooden spoon)*
*On my plate there (is/are) (some bread).*

# OPENING

### Circle time

**Materials and preparation**
- Audio library – songs
- Puppet
- Visual schedule pictures

Stand together in a circle and sing the *Hello song* (track 2). Say *hello* to the puppet and ask, *How are you?*
Remind students of the attention-getter, *1, 2, 3 It's time for... CBeebies!* Remind students that they should be quiet and pay attention whenever you say this.
Show the visual schedule pictures and invite the class helper to help you pick out the ones that represent what you will do today.

> **Note to teachers**
> Check on the watercress-growing experiment in the paper cups as a class. Allow students to compare the cups.

### Spoon race

**Materials and preparation**
- Spoons (x4)
- Rubber balls (x4)

Divide the class into four groups and stand in four lines at the front of the class. Give each student at the front of each line a spoon and a rubber ball. Students balance the ball on the spoon and race across to the other end of the classroom. Continue with the next four students in the line and until every student has raced.
You should set expectations of moving safely so as to avoid accidents.

# ACTIVE LEARNING

### Before watching the video – Talking about utensils

#### Materials and preparation
- Utensils: spoon, dessertspoon, teaspoon, wooden spoon, knife, fork, plate

Sit together in a circle and show each of the utensils one by one. Encourage students to mime using the utensils. Place the utensils in the middle of the circle. Call out the each utensil and invite individual students to take the correct utensil.

> **Note to teachers**
> Encourage students to notice the different sizes. You may like to bring in different utensils, e.g. plastic picnic utensils, metal ones, child-friendly ones, etc, and compare them.

### Watching the video – Let's watch!

#### Materials and preparation
- Video library

Sit together in a semicircle so everyone can see the screen. Play *Show Me Show Me, Series 4, Ep 20, Spoons & Ostriches* (Video 17). Watch the video together. Watch it again and stop at each different spoon featured and say what spoon it is and what size it is (*big* or *small*). Together, mime stirring and slurping from a spoon. You should set expectations of correct watching behavior, reminding students that they should sit still and watch quietly, respecting their classmates.

### After watching the video – Look, think, and draw.

#### Materials and preparation
- Crayons
- Pencils
- Project Book page 25

Sit students at their tables. Help them open their Project Books to page 25. Ask students what they can see and what's missing. Give students a pencil each and put the crayons in the middle of the table. Tell students to trace around the knife, fork, and spoon and color them. Then they draw their favorite food on the plate.

# DIFFERENTIATED INSTRUCTION

### BELOW LEVEL
#### Before watching the video
Focus only on *spoon* and *wooden spoon* and that one is for eating and the other one for stirring.

### ABOVE LEVEL
#### After watching the video
Have students analyze their plate and decide if it is healthy. Encourage them to add some healthy foods to the plate.

# CLOSING

### Compare your plates. Sing the *Goodbye song*.

#### Materials and preparation
- Audio library – songs
- Project Book page 25

Have students sit in groups or in pairs with their Project Book plate and compare their plates.
Sing the *Goodbye song* (track 3) and invite students to sing along while they put their things away. Encourage students to help each other and take responsibility for the classroom environment. Say *goodbye* to them and have them say *goodbye* back to you.

Unit 6 53

### Learning goals
- Talk about food items
- Identify ingredients and processes to make a cake

### Video objective
- Watch and follow a story in a video

### Main language content
Food: *birthday cake*
Cooking: *bake, mix, stir*
Ingredients: *baking powder, flour, milk, sugar*
We need (milk).
Let's (put it on the oven).

## OPENING

### Circle time

#### Materials and preparation
- Audio library – songs
- Puppet
- Visual schedule pictures

Stand together in a circle and sing the *Hello song* (track 2). Say hello to the puppet and ask, *How are you?* Everyone asks each other.
Remind students of the attention-getter, *Everybody look at me, it's time for CBeebies!* Remind students that they should be quiet and pay attention whenever you say this.
Show the visual schedule pictures and invite the class helper to help you pick out the ones that represent what you will do today.

> **Note to teachers**
> Together check on the watercress growing experiment in the paper cups. Allow students to compare the cups.

### Play *What am I eating?*

#### Materials and preparation
- Utensils: spoon, dessertspoon, teaspoon, wooden spoon, knife, fork, plate

Sit in a circle with students. Show the utensils one by one and elicit the names. Invite students to mime eating something; their classmates to guess what it is.

## ACTIVE LEARNING

### Before watching the video – How to make a birthday cake

**Materials and preparation**
- A large bowl
- Cake ingredients milk, flour, baking powder, eggs, sugar (play food or real)

Sit together in a circle. Show students the ingredients and elicit/teach the words. Ask, *Who knows how to make a cake?* Encourage students to tell you what order to put the ingredients in and how to make a simple cake. Mime adding the ingredients to the bowl, mixing, etc. Use the words, *mix, put in the oven,* and *bake* as you act it out.

> **Note to teachers**
> Ask students about their last birthday and what kind of cake they had.

### Watching the video - Let's watch!

**Materials and preparation**
- Video library

Sit together in a semicircle and make sure every student can see the screen. Play *Sarah and Duck Series 1, Ep 4, Cake Bake* (Video 18). Watch the video together. Watch the video again and stop to say the ingredients and mime the actions together. Stop and sing the video story birthday song. You should set expectations of correct watching behavior, reminding students that they should sit still and watch quietly, respecting their classmates.

### After watching the video – Look, color, and draw.

**Materials and preparation**
- Colored markers
- Glitter
- Glue
- Project Book page 27
- Ribbons
- Scissors

Sit students at their tables and put all the craft resources in the middle of the table. Help students open their Project Books to page 27. Ask, *What do you see?* Elicit, *A birthday cake!* Tell students to decorate the cake using any of the colors and decorations they like. Then they draw some candles.

> **Note to teachers**
> To help students with ideas, tell them it's a cake for Duck so they can all a picture of Duck.

## DIFFERENTIATED INSTRUCTION

### BELOW LEVEL
**Before watching the video**
Reduce the number of action words you use so as not to overwhelm students with new information.

### ABOVE LEVEL
**Before watching the video**
Invite students to think of other food items that you stir, mix, and bake in the oven.

## CLOSING

### Talk about the videos. Sing the *Goodbye song.*

**Materials and preparation**
- Audio library – songs

Talk with students about the three videos they watched in the unit. Encourage them to recall/act out what they saw in each video and say which was their favorite. Sing the *Goodbye song* (track 3) and invite students to sing along. Say *goodbye* to them and have them say *goodbye* back to you.

Unit 6 · 55

# Unit 7 How can farm animals help us?

**Learning goals**
- Understand what products animals produce
- Develop creative and motor skills in context

**Video objective**
- Use visuals to understand a video

**Main language content**
Clothing items: *woolen blanket, woolen hat, woolen socks*
Farm animals and products: *sheep (wool), cow (milk), chicken (egg)*
*Where does (wool) come from?*

## OPENING

### Circle time

**Materials and preparation**
- Audio library – songs
- Puppet
- Visual schedule pictures

Stand together in a circle and sing the *Hello song* (track 2). Say *hello* to the puppet and ask, *How are you?*
Remind students of the attention-getter, *Everybody look at me, it's time for CBeebies!* Remind students that they should be quiet and pay attention whenever you say this.
Show the visual schedule pictures and invite the class helper to help you pick out the ones that represent what you will do today.

> **Note to teachers**
> Try to extend the amount students contribute to Circle time and allow students to say what they think and feel.

### On the farm

**Materials and preparation**
- Printouts: sheep, cow, chicken, wool, milk, egg

Slowly reveal each of the animal pictures and mime them together. Ask students to guess and match the products with the animals. Stick the product pictures up around the classroom and stand together in the middle. Hold up an animal picture; students run to the correct product and say the word.
You should set expectations of walking safely so as to avoid accidents.

## ACTIVE LEARNING

### Before watching the video.

**Materials and preparation**

- A ball of wool
- Eggs (real or plastic)
- Milk (real or plastic)
- Pictures of different objects that are made from wool, eggs, and milk (optional)

Sit together in a circle. Show each item and ask students what it is. Then ask, *What animal does it come from?* Encourage them to say *sheep*, *chicken (hen)*, and *cow*. Invite students to think of things that they know that are made from these items, such as a woolly hat, an omelet, yogurt, etc.

> **Note to teachers**
> Show the pictures of different objects that are made from wool, eggs, and milk. Ask students to match them to the resource.

### Watching the video - Let's watch!

**Materials and preparation**

- Video library

Sit together in a semicircle so everyone can see the screen. Play *Kit & Pup*, *Series 1*, *Ep 38*, *Wool* (Video 19). Watch the video together. Watch it again and stop each time you see a sheep and an item made from wool. Say it together and mime putting on a hat and socks and covering yourself with a blanket.

You should set expectations of correct watching behavior, reminding students that they should sit still and watch quietly, respecting their classmates.

### After watching the video – Make socks with wool.

**Materials and preparation**

- A4 construction paper (one sheet per student)
- Glue
- Pencils
- Scissors (optional)
- Wool

Sit students at their tables and give each student a sheet of construction paper. Give students a pencil each and tell them to draw a big pair of socks. Put the wool, glue, and scissors in the middle of the table. Tell students to use the wool to cover and decorate the socks.

> **Note to teachers**
> Students can cut out the socks and use ribbon to tie them together.

## DIFFERENTIATED INSTRUCTION

### BELOW LEVEL
**On the farm**

Focus only on the sheep and the wool, without adding *cow*, *milk*, *chicken*, and *egg*. Recycle woolly items (*gloves* and *hat*) from previous units to further support students.

### ABOVE LEVEL
**On the farm**

Extend by inviting students to add as many other products as they can to the animal printouts and describe them to you.

## CLOSING

### Whose sock is this? Sing the *Goodbye song*.

**Materials and preparation**

- Audio library – songs
- Laundry basket
- Students' socks craft

Take all of students' sock crafts and place them in a laundry basket. Say, *Oh, no! Look at all these mismatched socks. Whose are they?* Pass the laundry basket around and invite students to take out a sock each. Encourage the student to describe the sock and hold it up for the owner to identify and collect.
Sing the *Goodbye song* (track 3) and encourage students to sing along. Say *goodbye* to them and have them say *goodbye* back to you.

**Learning goals**
- Talk about farm animals and the sounds they make
- Develop creative and motor skills in context
- Understand familiar words in a video

**Main language content**
Animal sounds: *moo, baa, cock-a-doodle-doo, neigh, quack*
Farm animals: *chicken, cow, duck, horse, sheep*

# OPENING

### Circle time

**Materials and preparation**
- Audio library – songs
- Puppet
- Visual schedule pictures

Stand together in a circle and sing the *Hello song* (track 2). Say *hello* to the puppet and ask, *How are you?*
Remind students of the attention-getter, *1, 2, 3 It's time for… CBeebies!* Remind students that they should be quiet and pay attention whenever you say this.
Show the visual schedule pictures and invite the class helper to help you pick out the ones that represent what you will do today.

> **Note to teachers**
> Remind students of the other attention-getters that they have learned.

### Sing *Old MacDonald*.

**Materials and preparation**
- Audio library – songs

Stand together in a circle and sing *Old MacDonald* (track 16). Mime the different animals and make the noises. Repeat and move around the room to allow students to practice.

## ACTIVE LEARNING

### Before watching the video – Animal sounds

#### Materials and preparation
- Flashcards: *chicken, cow, duck, horse, pig, sheep*

Sit together in a circle and slowly reveal each of the animal flashcards. Lay the cards out in front of the circle, say the name of the animal, and make the sound together. Mime and make the sound of one of the animals for students to guess. Invite students to mime and make the sound of an animal for the other students to guess.

> **Note to teachers**
> Animal sounds may vary in your students' L1 so allow students to make both and compare.

### Watching the video - Let's watch!

#### Materials and preparation
- Video library

Sit together in a semicircle so everyone can see the screen. Play *Yakka Dee, Series 3, Ep 13 Cow* (Video 20). Watch the video together. Watch it again and stop it to make the sound and ask about colors and sizes of the cows in the video.
You should set expectations of correct watching behavior, reminding students that they should sit still and watch quietly, respecting their classmates.

### After watching the video – Make a cow face mask.

#### Materials and preparation
- Colored markers
- Glue
- Paper plates (one per student)
- Popsicle sticks (one per student)
- Pink construction paper (cut into the shape of cows' noses)
- Scissors

Sit students at their tables and give each student a paper plate. Give each student a nose shape and elicit the word *nose*. Students stick the nose on their paper plates and then draw big eyes above the nose. Invite students to color their cow faces and stick on a popsicle stick to hold up their mask.

> **Note to teachers**
> It's difficult for students to cut out the eyes on a mask. It is easier for them to use a popsicle stick to hold up the mask and look around it rather than tie it around their heads and look through cut-out eyes.

## DIFFERENTIATED INSTRUCTION

### BELOW LEVEL
### Before watching the video

Focus only on *sheep*, *chicken*, and *cow*, as these are review words from the previous lesson Add only the sounds these animals make.

### ABOVE LEVEL
### After watching the video

Invite students to mingle around the classroom with their cow masks, introducing themselves, and making a cow sound.

## CLOSING

### Sing *Old MacDonald*. Say goodbye.

#### Materials and preparation
- Audio library – songs

Play *Old MacDonald* (track 16) and invite students to sing along while they clean up. When the song comes to the cow and cow sound part, have students hold up their cow masks and imitate the sound. Encourage students to help each other to put away the craft resources and take responsibility for the classroom environment. Sing the *Goodbye song* (track 3). Say *goodbye* to students and have them say *goodbye* back to you.

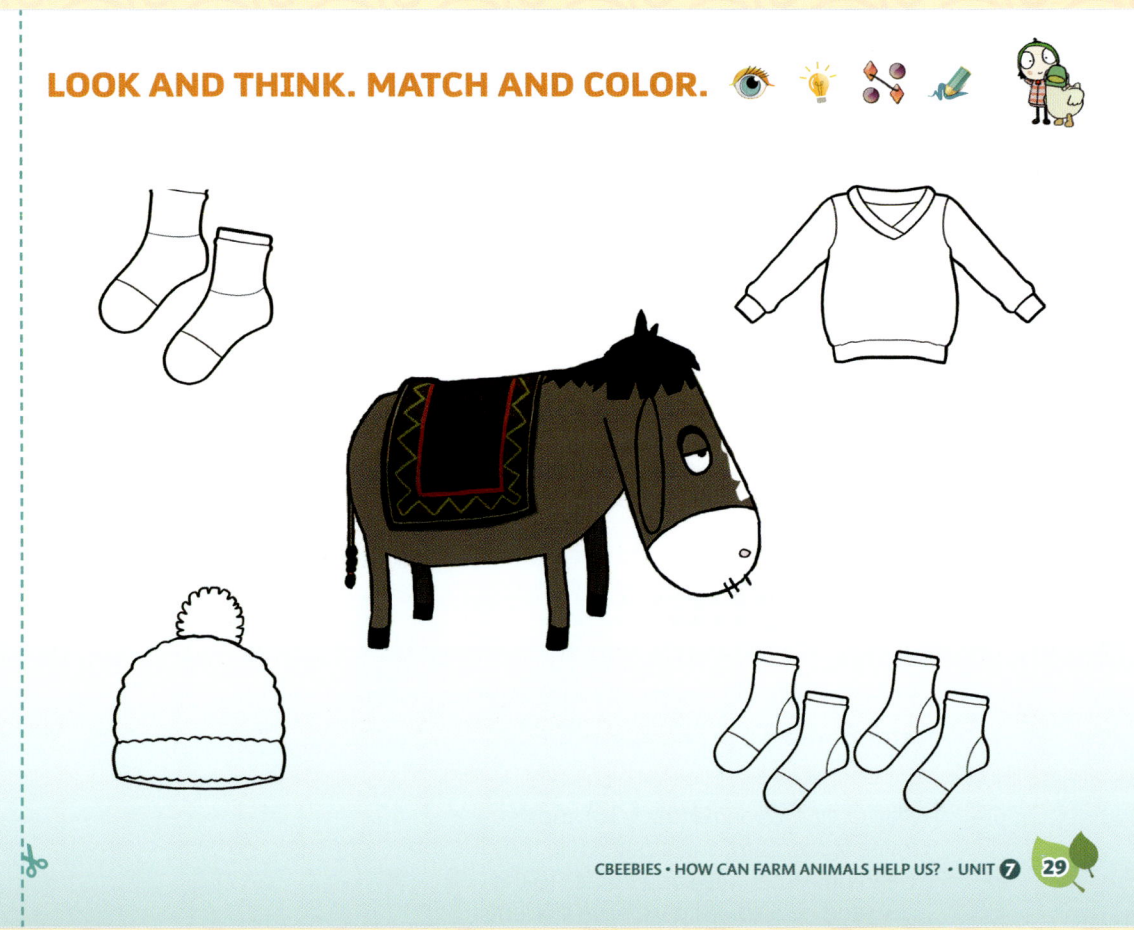

**Learning goals**
- Talk about woolen clothes and how they are done
- Develop creative and motor skills in context

**Main language content**
Knitting: knitting needles, wool, yarn
Woolen clothes: hat, scarf, socks, sweater

**Video objective**
- Watch and follow a story in a video

# OPENING

### Circle time

### Materials and preparation
- Audio library – songs
- Puppet
- Visual schedule pictures

Stand together in a circle and sing the *Hello song* (track 2). Say hello to the puppet and ask, *How are you?* Everyone asks each other.
Remind students of the attention-getter, *Everybody look at me, it's time for CBeebies!* Remind students that they should be quiet and pay attention whenever you say this.
Show the visual schedule pictures and invite the class helper to help you pick out the ones that represent what you will do today.

> **Note to teachers**
> Try and extend the amount students contribute to circle time and allow students to say what they think and feel.

### Sing Baa, baa black sheep.

### Materials and preparation
- Video of the nursery rhyme *Bah bah black sheep* (found on the Internet)

Stand together in a circle. Say the nursery rhyme together and mime the supporting actions, using audio or video to help you. Repeat and encourage students to join in and follow.

# ACTIVE LEARNING

### Before watching the video
### Materials and preparation
- Balls of yarn (wool)
- Knitting needles
- Woolen scarf

Sit together in a circle. Show students the yarn, knitting needles, and scarf. Ask students where wool comes from and if it keeps you cool or warm. Give each student some wool and together try finger knitting. To do finger knitting, students hold their hand out with their palms facing upwards. They hold the yarn between their thumb and forefinger, and then weave it under and over the other fingers. Then they loop back round and repeat. This is done several times. There are many helpful tutorials for finger knitting with kids on the Internet.

> **Note to teachers**
> Allow students some time to figure out and try finger knitting and don't worry too much about the final outcome.

### Watching the video – Let's watch!
### Materials and preparation
- Video library

Sit together in a semicircle and make sure every student can see the screen. Play *Sarah and Duck Series 3 Ep33 Whatsathingy?* (Video 21). Watch the video together. Watch the video again and stop to try to guess what each knitted part might be for. Stop at the end and ask students if they think Donkey is now happy and why.
You should set expectations of correct watching behavior, reminding students that they should sit still and watch quietly, respecting their classmates.

### After watching the video – Look and think. Match and color.
### Materials and preparation
- Crayons
- Project Bbook page 29
- Pencils

Sit students at their tables. Help them open their Project Books to page 29 and ask students what they can see (Donkey). As a group, ask what clothes Donkey was wearing in the video and on what body part. Students draw a line matching the clothes to Donkey's body part. Then they color the clothes.

> **Note to teachers**
> Fast finishers can work together and add background to the picture according to what they remember from the video.

# DIFFERENTIATED INSTRUCTION

### BELOW LEVEL
### After watching the video
Work together on finding and matching each part of the clothes on the donkey.

### ABOVE LEVEL
### After watching the video
### Materials and preparation
- Crayons
- Sheets of paper (one per student)

Once students have finished, give each student a sheet of paper and invite them to design and draw a wool outfit for Duck. Students can then show and share what they have designed.

# CLOSING

### Show and tell. Sing the *Goodbye song*.
### Materials and preparation
- Audio library – songs
- Project Book page 29

Have students sit in a circle and show each other their pictures. Encourage them to say what they like about their classmates' pictures.
Sing the *Goodbye song* (track 3) and invite students to sing along. Say *goodbye* to them and have them say *goodbye* back to you.

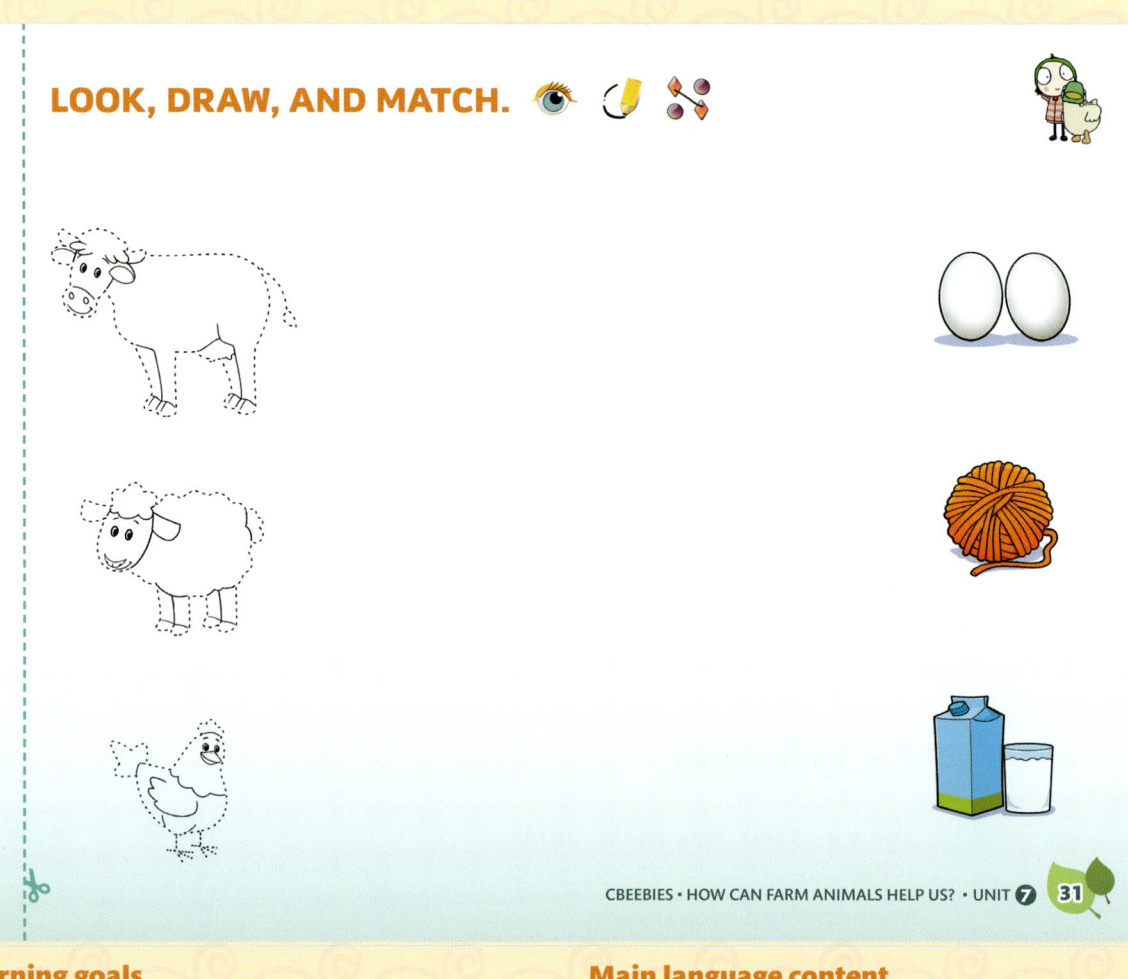

### Learning goals
- Understand what products animals produce
- Identify specific animals, their produce and function
- Give their opinion on a video

### Main language content
Animals: *chickens, cows, sheep*
Animal products: *eggs, milk, wool*
*(Chickens) give us (eggs).*
*We eat eggs. We drink milk.*
*Wool keeps us warm.*

# OPENING

### Circle time

### Materials and preparation
- Audio library – songs
- Puppet
- Visual schedule pictures

Stand together in a circle and sing the *Hello song* (track 2). Say hello to the puppet and ask, *How are you?* Everyone asks each other.
Remind students of the attention-getter, *Everybody look at me, it's time for CBeebies!* Remind students that they should be quiet and pay attention whenever you say this.
Show the visual schedule pictures and invite the class helper to help you pick out the ones that represent what you will do today.

> **Note to teachers**
> Try to extend the amount students contribute to circle time and allow students to say what they think and feel.

### Role-play *Baa, baa black sheep.*

### Materials and preparation
- Video of the nursery rhyme *Baa, baa black sheep* (found on the Internet)

Ask students if they remember *Baa, baa black sheep* from the previous class. Encourage them to recite it from memory. Play the audio/video and sing it together once. Then organize the class into groups and assign a different line of the rhyme to each group to say and act out.

## ACTIVE LEARNING

### Before watching the video – Look and match.

### Materials and preparation
- Egg carton
- Pictures or toys: of a cow, sheep, and chicken
- Play food (cake, eggs, milk)
- Milk carton
- Soda can
- Woolen scarf
- Yogurt pot

Sit together in a circle and show the animal pictures/toys. Ask, *What's this?* and elicit *cow, sheep, chicken*. Spread out the materials in the middle of the circle and encourage students to match them to the animals. Ask them if they can identify which item doesn't match any of the animals. (the soda can) Talk with them about the cake and help them realize that it matches both the cow (milk) and the chicken (egg).

> **Note to teachers**
> Encourage students to make the animal sounds as you show the pictures and say the words.

### Watching the video - Let's watch!

### Materials and preparation
- Video library

Sit together in a semicircle and make sure every student can see the screen. Play *Sarah and Duck Series 3 Ep33 Whatsathingy?* (Video 21). Watch the video again and stop to ask students how they got the wool, where it came from and how you make the outfit for Donkey. Ask students what other animal products they can see in the video.

You should set expectations of correct watching behavior, reminding students that they should sit still and watch quietly, respecting their classmates.

### After watching the video – Look, draw, and match.

### Materials and preparation
- Colored pencils
- Pencils
- Project Book page 31

Sit students at their tables. Help them open their Project Books to page 31 and ask them what they can see. Show students how to trace around each animal and then draw a line to the product that comes from that animal. Then students color the animals.

## DIFFERENTIATED INSTRUCTION

**BELOW LEVEL**
**After watching the video**

Students may not have time to color the animals. Tell them that they can do this at home.

**ABOVE LEVEL**
**After watching the video**

Students can draw things that they know are made of each product, e.g., ice cream (milk), an omelet, a sock, etc.

## CLOSING

### Talk about the videos. Sing the *Goodbye song*.

### Materials and preparation
- Audio library – songs

Talk with students about the three videos they watched in the unit. Encourage them to recall/act out what they saw in each video and say which was their favorite. Sing the *Goodbye song* (track 3) and invite students to sing along. Say *goodbye* to them and have them say *goodbye* back to you.

# Unit 8  Who lives and works in my town?

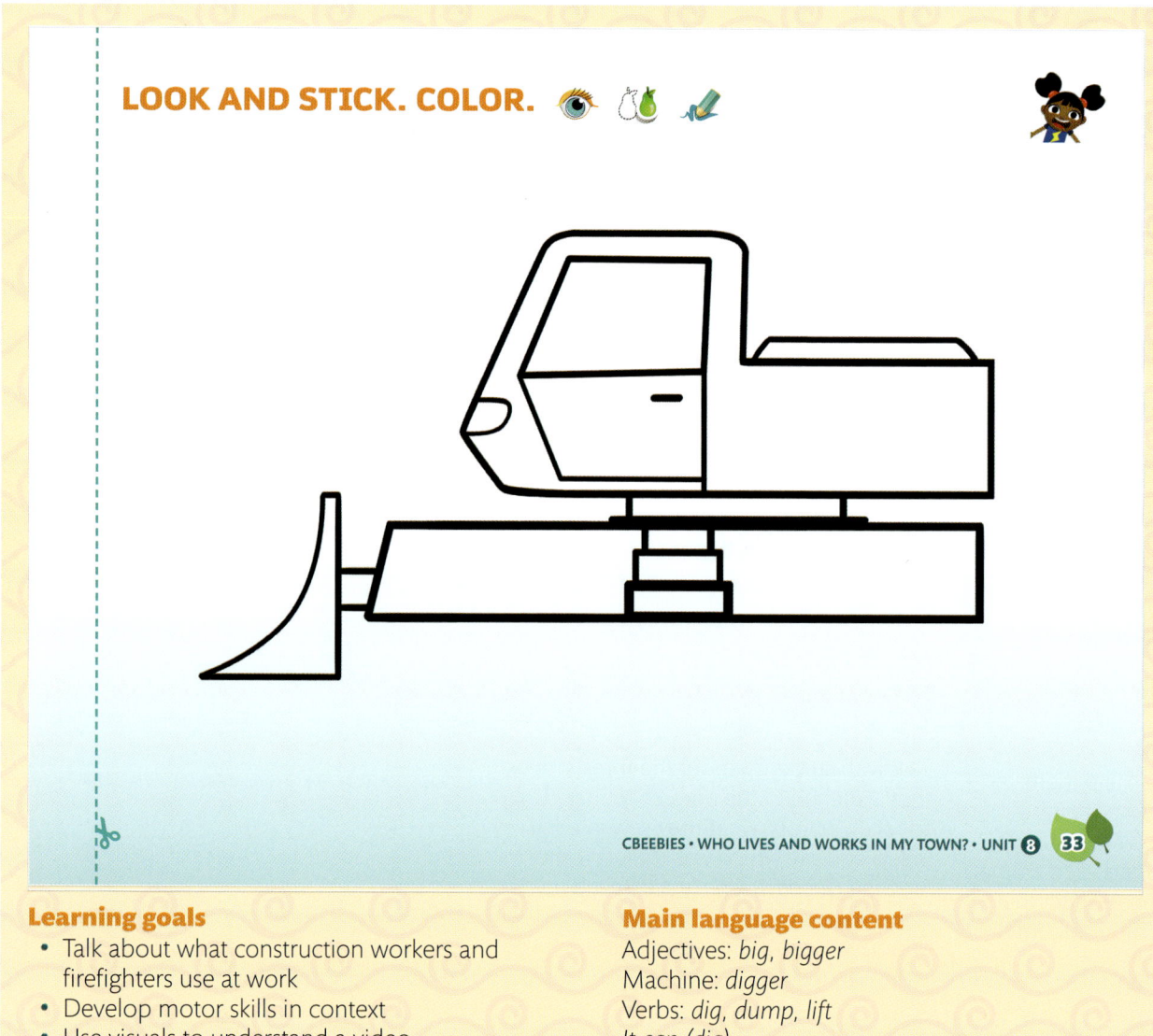

### Learning goals
- Talk about what construction workers and firefighters use at work
- Develop motor skills in context
- Use visuals to understand a video

### Main language content
Adjectives: *big, bigger*
Machine: *digger*
Verbs: *dig, dump, lift*
*It can (dig).*

## OPENING

### Circle time

**Materials and preparation**
- Audio library – songs
- Puppet
- Visual schedule pictures

Stand together in a circle and sing the *Hello song* (track 2). Say *hello* to the puppet and ask, *How are you?*
Remind students of the attention-getter, *Everybody look at me, it's time for CBeebies!* Remind students that they should be quiet and pay attention whenever you say this.
Show the visual schedule pictures and invite the class helper to help you pick out the ones that represent what you will do today.

> **Note to teachers**
> Try and extend the amount students contribute to Circle time and allow students to say what they think and feel.

### Play *Guess the shape.*

**Materials and preparation**
- Two whiteboard markers

Divide the class into two groups and stand them in a line facing the board. Give the first two students in each line a whiteboard marker. Use your finger to draw a circle on the back of the last two students in the lines. Those students do the same to the students in front of them. This continues until it reaches the first students in line, who draw what they felt on the board. Switch the order of students and repeat with other shapes or numbers.

CBeebies

# ACTIVE LEARNING

### Before watching the video – A digger digging

#### Materials and preparation
- A toy digger
- Sandbox and sand

Sit together in a circle and show students the digger. Ask, *What is it?* Say *digger* and encourage students to repeat. Invite them to tell you what a digger does. Then act out *digging, lifting,* and *dumping* using the toy digger and the sandpit. Invite students to try it out. Encourage them to say the words.

### Watching the video – Let's watch!

#### Materials and preparation
- Video library

Sit together in a semicircle so everyone can see the screen. Play *Yakka Dee, Series 3, Ep 9 Digger* (Video 22). Watch the video together. Watch it again and stop each time the digger performs one of the actions. Ask students to say and mime what they see. Highlight the words *big* and *bigger* from the video.
You should set expectations of correct watching behavior, reminding students that they should sit still and watch quietly, respecting their classmates.

### After watching the video – Look and stick. Color.

#### Materials and preparation
- Colored pencils
- Project Book page 33

Sit students at their tables. Help them open their Project Books to page 33 and ask they what they can see. Tell students that the need to complete the digger and help them find the stickers at the back of their Project Books. Help them with the stickers as needed. They stick the stickers in the correct places and then color the main digger cab.

> **Note to teachers**
> Fast finishers can add more background or surrounding detail to the page.

# DIFFERENTIATED INSTRUCTION

### BELOW LEVEL
**Before watching the video**
Focus on the single actions and words only – *dig, lift, dump,* without adding *It can* and without asking students to say the words. Students can mime or try out the actions.

### ABOVE LEVEL
**After watching the video**
Extend by asking students where a digger digs and why. Suggest reasons (to plant a tree, to build a house, and so on). Encourage students to draw details of the words on their Project Book pages and tell you about it.

# CLOSING

### Play *The digger game.* Sing the *Goodbye song.*

#### Materials and preparation
- Audio library – songs

Have students stand up. Call out the words *dig, lift, dump* one by one and have students pretend they are diggers doing these actions. Play some music. Students walk around in the circle. Call out one of the actions, e.g. *dig.* Students continue walking, but this time acting out digging. Continue in this way, alternating between the different actions. You should set out expectations of walking safely so as to avoid accidents.. Say *goodbye* to students and have them say *goodbye* back to you.

## OPENING

### Circle time

**Materials and preparation**
- Audio library – songs
- Puppet
- Visual schedule pictures

Stand together in a circle and sing the *Hello song* (track 2). Say *hello* to the puppet and ask, *How are you?*
Remind students of the attention-getter, *1, 2, 3 It's time for... CBeebies!* Remind students that they should be quiet and pay attention whenever you say this.
Show the visual schedule pictures and invite the class helper to help you pick out the ones that represent what you will do today.

> **Note to teachers**
> Remind students of the other attention-getters that they have learned.

### Vehicles in our town

**Materials and preparation**
- Pictures or toys: digger, fire engine, police car, digger, garbage truck

Sit together in a circle and show each of the pictures/toys. Say the words and invite students to mime driving them and making the corresponding sound. Organize the class into four groups and assign each group a vehicle to role-play the actions and drive the vehicle.

**Learning goals**
- Talk about what construction workers and firefighters use at work
- Understand the role of firefighters
- Explain understanding of a video

**Main language content**
Firefighters- and construction workers- related items: *blue light, digger, fire, fire engine (truck), hose, ladder, police car, garbage truck, siren*
*It's a (ladder).*

# ACTIVE LEARNING

### Before watching the video – What's in a fire truck?

**Materials and preparation**

- Large printout of a firefighter with a fire truck including a hose, ladder, and a blue light
- Toy fire truck (optional)

Sit in a circle with students and explore the picture. Point to the different elements (firefighter, firetruck, ladder, hose, blue light), say the words and help students understand the meaning. Talk with students about what fire fighters do. Ask prompting questions to help them understand that firefighters do an important job.

> **Note to teachers**
> If possible, show students a toy fire truck so they can see the way it is put together and where the different parts live.

### Watching the video – Let's watch!

**Materials and preparation**

- Video library

Sit together in a semicircle so everyone can see the screen. Play *Show Me Show Me, Series 3, Ep 6 Fire engines and Climbing* (Video 23). Watch the video together. Watch it again and stop it each time a part of the fire engine is shown, ask students what it is, and mime using it together.

You should set expectations of correct watching behavior, reminding students that they should sit still and watch quietly, respecting their classmates.

### After watching the video – Make a fire truck.

**Materials and preparation**

- Cardboard boxes (one per student for the fire truck)
- Glue
- Paints
- Red crepe paper
- Scissors

Sit students at their tables and put all the craft resources in the middle. Tell students you're going to make a fire truck; go over the parts that the fire truck has and ask about the color. Students paint and create their fire trucks.

> **Note to teachers**
> If you can't get enough cardboard boxes, create a fire truck template for students to color. Students can stick blue crepe paper for the siren and to simulate water coming out of the hose.

# DIFFERENTIATED INSTRUCTION

**BELOW LEVEL**
**Before watching the video**
Focus only on the digger and the fire engine to minimize the amount of new vocabulary and give students the opportunity to consolidate their understanding from the previous lesson.

**ABOVE LEVEL**
**After watching the video**
Extend by asking students to think of reasons why you need firefighters and fire trucks. During the video highlight and focus on the different tasks performed by the firefighters.

# CLOSING

### Playing with fire trucks. Sing the *Goodbye song*.

**Materials and preparation**

- Audio library – songs
- Students' fire trucks

Have students sit in a circle. Invite them to play together, acting out different situations.
Sing the *Goodbye song* (track 3) and invite students to sing along while they put their things away. Encourage students to help each other and put the craft resources back in the correct place. Say *goodbye* to them and have them say *goodbye* back to you.

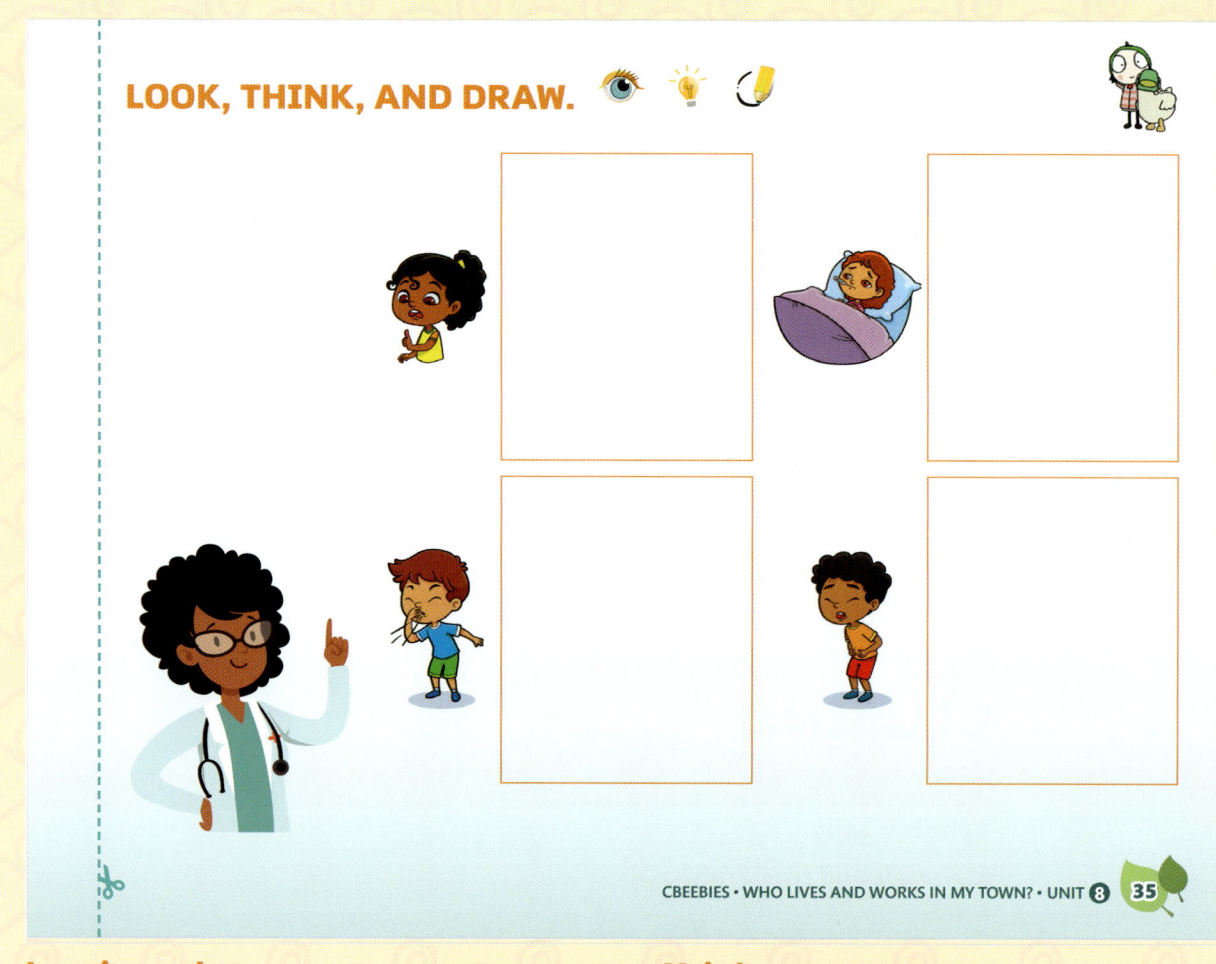

**Learning goals**
- Understand how nurses and doctors can help
- Recognize common illnesses

**Video objective**
- Understand an animated video

**Main language content**
Community helpers: *doctor, nurse*
Health problems: *fever, a cold, a cut, a stomachache*
*I have (a fever)*
*You need (medicine).*

# OPENING

### Circle time

### Materials and preparation
- Audio library – songs
- Puppet
- Visual schedule pictures

Stand together in a circle and sing the *Hello song* (track 2). Say *hello* to the puppet and ask, *How are you?*
Remind students of the attention-getter, *1, 2, 3 It's time for... CBeebies!* Remind students that they should be quiet and pay attention whenever you say this.
Show the visual schedule pictures and invite the class helper to help you pick out the ones that represent what you will do today.

> **Note to teachers**
> Remind students of the other attention-getters that they have learned.

### Mirror me

Divide the class into two groups. Group A and Group B. Line up the two groups up opposite each other. Group A can make any movement they want, and Group B mirrors the actions exactly. Then switch roles and have Group B make the movements.

CBeebies

## ACTIVE LEARNING

### Before watching the video – What's the matter?

**Materials and preparation**
- A bottle of water
- A pillow and a blanket
- Band-aids
- Tissues

Sit together in a circle. Mime having a fever, a stomachache, a cold, and a cut. Mime and say each condition together. Put the props in the middle of the circle. Mime the health conditions again and encourage students to match them to the props.

> **Note to teachers**
> Ask students if they've ever had any of the health conditions and ask what they did to help.

### Watching the video - Let's watch!

**Materials and preparation**
- Video library

Sit together in a circle and make sure every student can see the screen. Play *Sarah and Duck Series 1, Ep 16, Sarah gets a cold* (Video 24). Watch the video together. Watch the video again and stop to ask, **What is the matter with Sarah? Where is she going to get better?** Ask students what Duck does to help.
You should set expectations of correct watching behavior, reminding students that they should sit still and watch quietly, respecting their classmates.

### After watching the video – Look, think, and draw.

**Materials and preparation**
- Colored pencils
- Pencils
- Project Book page 35

Sit students at their table. Help them open their Project Books to page 35 and say what they can see. Ask student what each health condition needs to make it better and invite students to draw bottles of medicine or other items that make the conditions better.

## DIFFERENTIATED INSTRUCTION

### BELOW LEVEL
**Before watching the video**

Show pictures of each of the health conditions rather than just miming the actions in order to ensure students are clear on the meaning.

### ABOVE LEVEL
**Before watching the video**

Extend the activity by inviting students to think of other health conditions that you might get and where you might go to get better. Encourage them to mention hospitals, doctors, nurses, etc.

## CLOSING

### Role-play being doctors and nurses. Sing the *Goodbye song*.

**Materials and preparation**
- Audio library – songs
- Bandages and band-aids
- Selection of teddy bears (one per group of three or four students)
- Toy medical kits (optional, one per group of three or four students)

Sit in a circle with students and show them the teddy bears. Explain that they are sick, and invite students to say what might be wrong with them. Give out the toy medical kit and equipment (if available), and encourage students to role-play treating the teddy bears. If you don't have the medical kits, students can pretend to use medical instruments and to give medicine to the teddy bears.
Sing the *Goodbye song* (track 3) and invite students to sing along. Say *goodbye* to them nd have them say *goodbye* back to you.

### Learning goals
- Understand how nurses and doctors can help.
- Identify and make suggestions on how to feel better

### Video objective
- Explain understanding of a video

### Main language content
Community helpers: *doctor, nurse*
Health problems: *fever, a cold, a cut, a stomachache*
*I have (a fever).*
*You need (medicine).*

## OPENING

### Circle time

**Materials and preparation**
- Audio library – songs
- Puppet
- Visual schedule pictures

Stand together in a circle and sing the *Hello song* (track 2). Say *hello* to the puppet and ask, *How are you?*
Remind students of the attention-getter, *Everybody look at me, it's time for CBeebies!* Remind students that they should be quiet and pay attention whenever you say this.
Show the visual schedule pictures and invite the class helper to help you pick out the ones that represent what you will do today.

> **Note to teachers**
> Try to extend the amount students contribute to Circle time and allow students to say what they think and feel.

### What's wrong?

Sit together in a circle. Mime an illness from the previous lesson and students guess what's wrong. Invite students to think about what you can do to get better. Invite students to mime their idea for the rest of the class to guess.

## ACTIVE LEARNING

### Before watching the video – What is it?

**Materials and preparation**
- Printouts - medicine, bandage, rest, doctor, nurse

Sit together in a circle. Slowly reveal each of the printouts. Mix up the pictures, say an illness, and students show and tell you what you need to get better.. Stick the pictures up around the classroom. In groups, students go to each picture, mime the problem, and say the solution together.

> **Note to teachers**
> Focus on students' concept recognition more than language production.

### Watching the video – Let's watch!

#### Materials and preparation
- Video library

Sit together in a semicircle and make sure every student can see the screen. Play *Sarah and Duck Series 1, Ep 16, Sarah gets a cold* (Video 24). Watch the video together. Watch the video again and stop to ask students what is wrong with Sarah and Duck at the end. Ask students what Duck does in the doctor's office.
You should set expectations of correct watching behavior, reminding students that they should sit still and watch quietly, respecting their classmates.

### After watching the video – Role-play at the doctors

#### Materials and preparation
- Toys/props related to doctors and nurses

Divide the class into four groups.
Make each corner of the room into a mini-doctor's office and assign one group to each corner. Tell students they are going to role-play being at the doctors'. Two students play being sick, and two students are a doctor or a nurse.

> **Note to teachers**
> If there is time, invite some groups to perform their role-play for the rest of the class.

## DIFFERENTIATED INSTRUCTION

### BELOW LEVEL
### After watching the video

Assign clear roles and give the students who are sick a specific condition to mime. Support with pictures up on the board for every student to see and help with offering solutions.

### ABOVE LEVEL
### After watching the video

Invite students to suggest alternative solutions to the condition and encourage students to use full phrases.

## CLOSING

### Talk about the videos. Sing the *Goodbye song.*

#### Materials and preparation
- Audio library – songs

Talk with students about the three videos they watched in the unit. Encourage them to recall/act out what they saw in each video and say which was their favorite. Sing the *Goodbye song* (track 3) and invite students to sing along. Say *goodbye* to them and have them say *goodbye* back to you.

# Notes

# Notes

# Notes

# Notes

# Notes

# Notes

# Notes

# Notes

# Notes